The Collective

Essays on Reality

Michele Doucette

The Collective: Essays on Reality

ISBN 978-1-935786-04-7

Printed in the United States of America by

St. Clair Publications

PO Box 726

McMinnville, TN 37111-0726

http://stanstclair.net

Acknowledgments

All truths are easy to understand once they are discovered; the point is to discover them.

These very words, attributed to Galileo, are profound in their simplicity.

Who looks outside, dreams; who looks inside, awakes.

Carl Gustav Jung said it all with this brief statement.

I think we all have a little voice inside us that will guide us. If we shut out all the noise and clutter from our lives and listen to that voice, it will tell us the right thing to do.

My favorite remembrance of Christopher Reeve was his portrayal of Richard Collier, a playwright who became smitten by a photograph of a young woman at the Grand Hotel on Mackinac Island, in the 1980 romantic fantasy, *Somewhere In Time*. These particular words of his seem even more pertinent to me now.

Table of Contents

Reviews

The first word that comes to mind is Bravo. I do not know anyone (other than you) who has gone through the steps of getting out of the Matrix by turning off all (or most) external stimulus and turning on the sixth sense.

While I am unfamiliar with the work of Ivan Fraser, he is certainly aware of how the world currently works. Having read most of David Icke's work, I believe his writing to be most accurate (at least 95%). That having been said, you have encapsulated the issues quite nicely.

All this to say that what you are doing, and have done, is quite commendable. Already knowing everything that you have stated in your essays, I have never disengaged as you have. I still watch TV, read newspapers, read magazines, but I do this standing behind the short wall, so to speak, even though I know this is the longer route to take. Your method is the faster for sure!

Jean-Guy Poirier, Canada

The second paragraph on page 67 says it all, with clarity and simplicity.

If we want change for the better, we need to understand first what we have to deal with, and secondly that real change will not come from the top down, but rather from the bottom up which clearly means that, in order to be in control of our lives, we must also take responsibility for ourselves. Collectively, all are responsible for the current state of affairs.

I am humbled by both your depth as well as your spiritual conviction.

Elio Serra, USA

I just read your essays; very good, well done; it's exactly my perception. Yes, yes, yes, your first essay is precisely what I've been trying to pass along to others. Believe me, those who are in control tried to take my life from me at one point. I stood my ground and with the help of love from the Source of ALL, I survived.

David Shirk, USA

Tell me that you are planning to publish this somewhere. This collection of essays is simply EXCELLENT. In fact, I think this may possibly be your best writing yet!

Nannette Blondet, USA

I have just completed *From Science to God: A Physicist's Journey into the Mystery of Consciousness* by Peter Russell. In addition, I have just ordered *Physics of the Impossible: A Scientific Exploration into the World of Phasers, Force Fields, Teleportation and Time Travel* by Michio Kaku. Needing to be read in conjunction with each other, they both touch on some of the ideas in this book, albeit from a scientific view. It seems you have found your way (via a different path) to many of the same conclusions as these scientists. I see that as being very good.

Reading about the *Brotherhood* has been more than a little disconcerting for me because I have had extremely deep and animated discussions with both Muslim and Hindu friends about the Brotherhood of Islam. This particular Brotherhood consists of a bunch of thugs and terrorists trying to unite all the world into an 'ulma', surrounding and strangling and forcing the world to accept extreme Islam.

I am also able to recall a book I read, years ago, in Thailand. Called *Lords of the Rim*, it discussed the Chinese version of the Illuminati, one that began over a thousand years ago with the "twelve heavenly kings" whose descendents have carried on their secret pact ever since. *Lords of the Rim* refers to the Pacific Rim whereby they had their bases on mainland China and launched trade ships worldwide, setting up small trade centers on a global basis. They, too, plan to eventually close the noose and have the world under their financial dominion.

It is clear, then, that each has both an agenda with something resembling an Illuminati Brotherhood. Who is it that shall ultimately win? Chances are, we may not live long enough to know that answer, unless, of course, the Apocalypse occurs in our lifetime.

Thank you for letting me have this "sneak preview". This is a very well written composition, Michele. I continue to wish you every success on your journey.

Suzanne Olsson, author of *Jesus in Kashmir: The Lost Tomb*

Our Current Collective Reality Is Most Shocking Indeed

© July 2007 by Michele Doucette

The material you are about to delve into may cause many to become more fearful of the current collective reality.

I have been told that this piece is one of my best, that I should seek publication.

I have also been told that the writing style employed throughout could be viewed as both my greatest strength and my greatest weakness in that I am relying on others to identify the problem, thereby providing their answers.

I prefer to let the reader decide for themselves.

My intent in composing this essay has been merely to better *inform the reader*, so that all of us can work on actively disengaging from the Matrix.

Personal experience dictates that I must first acknowledge what appears to be happening before I am able to work toward becoming master of my body, master of my mind and master of my emotions.

Thinking leads to questions and questions lead to knowledge. It becomes imperative that each reader conduct his or her own research and investigation into the so-called reality of their existence.

This is a process that involves much inner reflection, for it is only in the discovery of the real Self that one begins to awaken.

Seek so that ye may find.

In 1610, Galileo published an account of his telescopic observations of the moons of Jupiter, using such to argue in favor of the Copernican heliocentric (sun-centered) theory of the universe.

In doing so, he was going against the dominant geocentric (earth-centered) Ptolemaic and Aristotelian theories strongly supported by the Catholic Church.

Opposition in 1612 led to a 1614 denouncing of Galileo's opinions on the motion of the earth, judging them close to heresy.

In 1616, Galileo received an admonition from Cardinal Bellarmino that he was neither to advocate, nor teach, Copernican astronomy.

Continuing his study of astronomy, Galileo became more and more convinced that all of the planets revolved around the sun, publishing a book in 1632 that stated, among other things, that the heliocentric theory of Copernicus was correct.

Called before the Inquisition, this time Galileo was found guilty of heresy. Although sentenced to life imprisonment in 1633, this was later commuted to house arrest due to age and poor health.

As implausible as this may seem, the incredible mind of Galileo, the *father of modern astronomy*, the *father of modern physics*, the *father of science*, was deemed a heretic for the simple reason that he held to a non-conformist opinion which opposed that enforced by the Roman Catholic Church.

For heresy to exist, there must be an authoritative system of dogma designated as orthodox (correct theological observance as determined by some overseeing body).

Having completed my Masters of Education (Literacy) in July 2006, I am now finding that I am having a difficult time with any type of authoritative system that attempts to dictate what I must believe, what I am to think, how I must act and what I must teach my children.

One's experience of life can only be determined by the framework that surrounds the society of which they are a part, a framework that shapes every aspect of their lives, be it through culture, education, health care, religion, media and science, to name but a few societal components.

Regardless of how the framework came to be imposed, the truth is that "the same attitudes control education, media, governments and banks and therefore exert an irrepressible influence over every aspect of our lives, our thoughts and opinions." [1]

Fraser goes further to share that "this framework has not been constructed by chance or appeared by accident. It is a deliberate policy which has been implemented over the centuries and continues with ever more sinister repercussions today." [2]

A deliberate policy with sinister repercussions?

Now that was something that grabbed my attention. Given that I am no longer willing to obtain information "from the mainstream media that sells you the daily falsehoods on which you decide what to think and believe," [3] courtesy of my Masters program, it may well be that Fraser is right.

I endeavored to find out more about this *deliberate* policy.

The distinction between *esoteric* knowledge (available only to initiates) and *exoteric* knowledge (available to all) has long been a part of the religious life of man. This means that

---

[1] Fraser, Ivan. "The Brotherhood and the Manipulation of Society". The Truth Campaign magazine. December 1996: Volume 3, p 16.
[2] Ibid.
[3] Icke, David. (2005). *Infinite Love is the Only Truth – Everything Else is Illusion* (p 1). Wildwood, MO: Bridge of Love Publications USA.

esoteric knowledge has been largely withheld from the majority, of which most belong, myself included.

The secrecy involved in such an undertaking is what apparently led to the formation of a variety of mystery schools. "Secrecy was maintained by these orders to avoid persecution and to prevent the very powerful information from falling into the hands of those who would use it for imbalanced reasons." [4]

It is my understanding that these mystery schools began to lose sight of "the original purity of their doctrines," [5] something that does not bode well for genuine enlightenment seekers of this day and age. As a result, it has been within some of these very secretive bodies, those that continue to exist today, that "the Luciferic consciousness has managed to take hold with disastrous consequences for mankind." [6] To further clarify, Fraser refers to the Luciferic consciousness as a "general term to describe the state of mind which created the historical global state of negative imbalance." [7]

---

[4] Fraser, Ivan. "The Brotherhood and the Manipulation of Society". The Truth Campaign magazine. December 1996: Volume 3, p 16.
[5] Ibid.
[6] Ibid, p 17.
[7] Ibid, p 16.

In short, it is a mindset which encompasses fear, guilt, lust for power, greed, envy, jealousy, all very much a part of the current societal framework "engineered throughout the ages by these imbalanced secret societies in order to perpetuate their wealth and power." [8]

Finally, it felt as if I was on to something that might lead to this *deliberate* policy that Fraser had been referencing.

"Armed with vast amounts of wealth and esoteric knowledge, the negative secret society network has flourished as the *aristocracy* [my italics] of the world. Power, wealth and information has been gained and maintained via warfare, exploitation, and especially in the last century, through control of the world's economic systems. Collectively, these organisations, led by the self-appointed global Elite, have become known as the *Brotherhood.*" [9] In keeping, "the only way for the Brotherhood to prosper is to keep the world in ignorance of who they really are. Power always seeks power and will

---

[8] Fraser, Ivan. "The Brotherhood and the Manipulation of Society". The Truth Campaign magazine. December 1996: Volume 3, p 16.
[9] Ibid.

never stop until all power is focused solely in the hands of the most ambitious." [10]

My intuition was telling me that there was much truth to these words. The next step, of course, involved attempting to identify *who* Fraser was targeting in keeping with this Brotherhood.

"In the last century, with the acceleration in technological development, particularly in terms of communication, the Elite have sought to realize their ambitions more swiftly with more blatant and definable aims: (1) the creation of a World Government, (2) a world currency and bank, (3) a world army, (4) the control of public opinion culminating in a micro-chipped population connected to a central computer, (5) the destruction of any alternatives to the System, and (6) to make large amounts of money in the process. This sinister plan by the Elite has become popularly known by researchers as the *New World Order*," [11] with their aim being to create a centralised fascist state by way of the aforementioned means.

---

[10] Fraser, Ivan. "The Brotherhood and the Manipulation of Society". The Truth Campaign magazine. December 1996: Volume 3, p 16.
[11] Ibid.

Although the term New World Order is not unknown to me, I had never taken the time to conduct research into all that was deemed to be part of this global initiative.

According to Fraser, these global Elite individuals have "allowed themselves to become slaves to, and also the major implementers of, the Luciferic consciousness which has taken this planet to the brink of destruction." [12]

In further addressing this Brotherhood, "the top level members ... are among the richest, and most powerfully influential people in the world. They are also responsible, directly and indirectly, for most of the money/power based crimes such as the illegal drug industry, political assassinations, Satanism and mind control which goes on every day, all around the world." [13]

To be more explicit, this Brotherhood, known collectively as the Illuminati or 'Illuminated Ones', "manipulate through secret societies and groups like Freemasons, Knights of Malta, Knights Templar and the Jesuits. These and others feed carefully chosen recruits into the Illuminati and they are

---

[12] Fraser, Ivan. "The Brotherhood and the Manipulation of Society". The Truth Campaign magazine. December 1996: Volume 3, p 18.
[13] Ibid.

installed in positions of power throughout the world, infesting all colours, races, creeds and countries." [14]

I was shocked to see the Freemasons, Knights of Malta, Knights Templar and the Jesuits collectively linked to this Illuminati Brotherhood.

However, after delving into Fraser's research, at least ten years in the making, what he shares *is* plausible.

"At the apex of the Brotherhood are the select few who actually know the *full* agenda. All other members (nearly five million worldwide) are ignorant of the true purpose of their individual organisation as a front for the Illuminati. Only the most suitable are selected to rise in the ranks, those recognized as being wealthy, ambitious and corrupt enough to perpetuate the ultimate goal which is world dominion. Everyone else provides a front, a smoke screen of ignorance and misinformation and all must offer complete obedience to the will of their organization." [15]

Suffice it to say that I am aghast to learn, *should this be true*, that nearly five million persons are being deceived as to the

---

[14] Icke, David. (2003). *Tales from the Time Loop* (p 35). Wildwood, MO: Bridge of Love Publications USA.
[15] Fraser, Ivan. "The Brotherhood and the Manipulation of Society". The Truth Campaign magazine. December 1996: Volume 3, p 18.

fraudulent purpose(s) behind the very organizations of which they believe they are a significant and important part.

"Betrayal of the Brotherhood is the worst crime possible in the eyes of its members and is ultimately punishable by death." [16]

Given their true purpose, as highlighted thus far, this goes without saying, does it not?

"The Brotherhood owns the law, they own the military, they own the oil companies, pharmaceutical companies and just about everything which provides fuel for the status quo. It sets the standards for education, it sets the curriculum, it plants seeds via the media and education systems of what will later become, through tender nurturing, power hungry, dissatisfied, spiritually unaware slaves to their System." [17]

I find it most frightening to realize that it is this very Brotherhood that has *created* the societal framework that we subscribe to, as per our culture, education, health care, religion, media and science, thereby being responsible for *orchestrating* the very lives that we lead.

---

[16] Fraser, Ivan. "The Brotherhood and the Manipulation of Society". The Truth Campaign magazine. December 1996: Volume 3, p 18.
[17] Ibid, pp 18-19.

No doubt about it, it appears that we are truly living in the Matrix.

"Political systems are also a front for the Brotherhood elite. Not as representatives of the people, elected by the people, for the people, but as tools of and for", you guessed it, "the Brotherhood". In addition, "science is controlled to the benefit of the elite, wars are created and manipulated to the benefit of the elite." [18]

As awful as this may sound, "every time a bomb is dropped or a tank built, ultimately it is the multi-national businesses who profit, especially the oil industries and world bankers. The scale of the manipulation in all areas of the status quo is almost immeasurable and for this reason virtually unbelievable to most prisoners of the System." [19]

Can this *really* be true?

Is *everything* controlled by this Brotherhood? Are we *truly* prisoners to a System that dictates what we must believe, what we are to think, how we must act and what we must teach our children?

---

[18] Fraser, Ivan. "The Brotherhood and the Manipulation of Society". The Truth Campaign magazine. December 1996: Volume 3, p 19.
[19] Ibid.

For fans of the Matrix trilogy, it is not as far fetched as it may seem, and, therefore, requires further delving into. This is why there is a chapter dedicated solely to unplugging from the Matrix in my book, *The Ultimate Enlightenment For 2012: All We Need Is Ourselves.*

"Since Babylonian times usury, the lending of wealth at interest, has been one of the main causes of war and empire building. Nations such as Persia and Rome became great due to their massive debts incurred by lending money from wealthy nations. Later, unable to return the wealth, but rich with great armies funded by this borrowed wealth, they soon realized a need to conquer these lending nations in order to nullify their debts. This was also the reason for the introduction of taxes, a global system which is in use right up to today." [20]

With respect to the Third World countries, these private companies, the banks, would rather keep these nations in debt for the simple reason that they "need to borrow money to produce goods to sell to other nations in order to raise the money to pay back the banks at interest whilst their people starve and die. Many researchers have come to conclude that this is a *deliberate* policy of the Illuminati to destroy the

---

[20] Fraser, Ivan. "The Brotherhood and the Manipulation of Society". The Truth Campaign magazine. March 1997: Volume 4, p 11.

poorer nations through famine, disease and manipulated war in order to take total control of their lands." [21]

Of course, the penalty for not being able to repay one's debt is forfeiture of property and land. The lands of the so-called Third World countries are often rich in mineral wealth, all in keeping with the *deliberate* policy that has been established by Fraser.

"In reality, very few people are almost entirely responsible for the vast majority of negativity and suffering in the world. It is an ingenious system which has all at its mercy. The great god *Banking*, together with its spin off deities of *Economic Growth* and *Gross Domestic Product* has seen to it that the majority of the world's nations are drowning in an ocean of debt whilst the minority elite are floating on staggering amounts of wealth." [22]

Whilst equating Banking, Economic Growth and Gross Domestic Product with deity status may come across as being very sarcastic, what Fraser discloses here is true.

"It makes little secret of its origins either: the symbol of the Illuminati for the Brotherhood, the 'All Seeing Eye' which

[21] Fraser, Ivan. "The Brotherhood and the Manipulation of Society". The Truth Campaign magazine. March 1997: Volume 4, p 12.
[22] Ibid.

sits inside a triangle/pyramid, is the symbol which adorns the U.S. dollar bill." [23]

The information presented herein is not meant to scare, but rather to enlighten so that all can make a more informed decision as to how to further proceed with their lives.

"It is easier to *know* the truth than to *live* the truth. However, it is only possible to live in truth when one knows the truth. Therefore, it should be our prime responsibility to seek truth. To know the truth is the key to freedom. To live in truth is to live in harmony." [24]

Taking this one step further, "those that live in truth are like shining beacons to those who have not yet discovered the reality of truth or are afraid to live in the light of truth, because of external pressures." [25]

---

[23] Fraser, Ivan. "The Brotherhood and the Manipulation of Society". The Truth Campaign magazine. March 1997: Volume 4, p 12.
[24] Fraser, Ivan. "The Paramount Necessity for Truth". The Truth Campaign magazine. June 1997: Volume 5, p 4.
[25] Ibid.

In addition, "to live in truth and to speak one's truth benefits all of us and empowers those who find it difficult to do this." [26]

All can aspire to become truth, to live truth, especially where "the human condition today, which sees a prevalence of negativity, in diverse forms such as hatred, greed, lust, envy, deliberate infliction of pain and distress, the direct result of being out of balance with truth" [27] is so profoundly widespread.

In essence, "the more people make the choice to live in truth, love and harmony, the easier it will be for others to gravitate towards that state." [28]

And now for the ultimate message. "No one is going to heal the planet for us. *The planet will be healed when we heal ourselves* [my italics]. Health lies within the zone of balance along with love and truth. All disease is an indication of imbalance and a lesson in rebalancing by bringing ourselves back into line with truth and love." [29]

---

[26] Fraser, Ivan. "The Paramount Necessity for Truth". The Truth Campaign magazine. June 1997: Volume 5, p 4.
[27] Ibid, p 5.
[28] Ibid.
[29] Ibid.

To be successful in this endeavor, "we need to educate ourselves and immerse ourselves in truth." [30]

Although I had never given it much thought before, what Fraser next shares is mind blowing.

"The best way to pass a lie into conventional know is to sandwich it between two truths; that it may not be noticed and it will be accepted as truth. And the best way to discredit a truth is to pass it off between two lies. We must be aware of these tactics in this age of information overload and active disinformation distribution." [31]

As we are coming to know, "the most effective tactic of the New World Order is to *divide and rule*. Divide people on the basis of religious ideology, wealth, politics, physical location ... remove their local power base to a central power base. The real power to benefit from all of this division lies with those who pull the strings and rebuild order from chaos (*which they themselves created*) in the fashion that they desired all along." [32]

---

[30] Fraser, Ivan. "The Paramount Necessity for Truth". The Truth Campaign magazine. June 1997: Volume 5, p 5.
[31] Ibid.
[32] Ibid.

Once again, the *deliberate* policy appears to have been unveiled.

The testimony by Cathy O'Brien and Mark Phillips, in their book *Trance-Formation of America*, gives copious amounts of substantiated support to the view that "we are living in an age of immense importance whereby the outcome of the battle between light and dark will be decided by our understanding and application of Truth." [33]

"Truth as *light* can be used to directly counteract the darkness. Unless you can be in active control of your thoughts in the light of truth then there is a force which *will* control your thoughts and reality by using the darkness of untruth." [34]

All energy seeks balance. As a continuance to this line of thinking, I, too, am of the same views as Fraser when he writes that "the sooner we begin to work for truth with the same fervor that the 'opposition' pursue their agenda, the sooner we will have global peace and therefore be enabled to evolve into boundless creativity and love." [35]

---

[33] Fraser, Ivan. "The Paramount Necessity for Truth". The Truth Campaign magazine. June 1997: Volume 5, p 6.

[34] Ibid.

[35] Ibid.

There are many on the planet today who both know and feel that we are in the midst of a great transformation in consciousness.

It is this very metamorphosis that shall take "us out of the prevailing state of negative imbalance and into a harmonious existence which has not been experienced on our planet for millennia. We are emerging from a long period of suppression and control into a new age of freedom." [36]

In keeping with this transmutation, "the old dark way of fear, lies and desire for control are being removed in favor of love, truth and co-operation with our fellow planetary beings whereby we have now reached the zenith of our collective experience and decided that enough is enough. It is time for change. And change we must if we are to have any kind of future worth fighting for." [37]

This change is now "looming from *within* individuals all around the world who are rejecting the values imposed through manipulation. An awakening of consciousness and an opening up to spirituality is occurring on a massive scale. This is the latest stage in the evolution of mankind which

[36] Fraser, Ivan. "Beyond the Veil". The Truth Campaign magazine. December 1977: Volume 7, p 31.
[37] Ibid.

will see the old dark ways removed in preparation for an age when light and harmony will prevail." [38]

The Hopi, also known as "The Peaceable People", a Native American nation, believe that we are currently in between the end of the fifth world (completed in 1987) and the beginning of the sixth (to begin in 2012).

They refer to this time between worlds as the Apocalypse or Revelation, a time of the revealing of truth. It has been foretold that the completion of this "time between worlds" will bring regeneration to the planet in that Mother Earth, a living entity, will transcend to another level (frequency or consciousness) and a new and special era will begin, a time for all things positive.

The times are here for total brotherhood, unlike the current and prevalent mindset which "actively seeks to keep from you the knowledge which is yours by Divine right; a knowledge which will set us free of the bonds we have imposed on ourselves." [39]

"In order to escape the prison we have built for ourselves through conceding our power to those who have set

---

[38] Fraser, Ivan. "Beyond the Veil". The Truth Campaign magazine. December 1977: Volume 7, p 31.
[39] Ibid.

themselves up as our 'superiors' we must first regain the knowledge which we have lost." [40]

"As long as we are prepared to stand aside and allow others to think for us and to provide the answers, we will forever be under the control of those who are prepared to exploit us for their own ends. Only through individuals working on their own spiritual development, taking direct responsibility for their lives and the consequences of their actions will things begin to improve. In order to heal the world we must first heal ourselves." [41]

A most powerful message, indeed.

Change must begin, first and foremost, within each and every individual.

If I may reflect further, David Icke also refers to a plan called the Brotherhood Agenda whereby a few are cleverly manipulating the entire planet through the "globalisation of business, banking and communications. The foundation of that control has always been the same: keep the people in ignorance, fear and at war with themselves. Divide, rule and

---

[40] Fraser, Ivan. "Beyond the Veil". The Truth Campaign magazine. December 1977: Volume 7, p 31.
[41] Ibid.

conquer while keeping the most important knowledge to yourself." [42]

In Icke's words, the global fascist state is already here. And yet, he continues, "it doesn't have to be like this. The real power is with the many, not the few. Indeed, infinite power is within every individual. The reason we are so controlled is not that we don't have the power to decide our own destiny, it is that we give that power away every minute of our lives." [43]

How, then, have the few managed to control the many for so long?

By way of emotional and mental mind control.

Taking it one step further, Icke says that physical control "is not necessary when you can manipulate the way people think and feel to the point where they 'decide' to do what you want them to do anyway and demand that you introduce laws that you want to introduce." [44]

_____

[42] Icke, David. (1999). *The Biggest Secret* (p xi). Scottsdale, AZ: Bridge of Love Publications USA.
[43] Ibid, pp xi-xii.
[44] Ibid, p xii.

In keeping, when you look at the definition of mind control as being "the manipulation of someone's mind so that they think, and therefore act, the way you want them to," [45] it becomes clear that this is what has been happening for at least the last several thousand years.

"They want your mind because when they have that, they have you. The answer lies in taking our minds back, thinking for ourselves and allowing others to do the same without fear of ridicule or condemnation for the crime of being different." [46]

In summation, Icke is saying that if we regain control of our minds, thereby achieving mental sovereignty, the Brotherhood Agenda cannot come to fruition.

In further referencing the Brotherhood, they are "a race of interbreeding bloodlines, a race within a race in fact, that were centered in the Middle and Near East in the ancient world and, over the thousands of years since, have expanded their power across the globe. A crucial aspect of this has been to create a network of mystery schools and secret societies to covertly introduce their Agenda while, at

---

[45] Icke, David. (1999). *The Biggest Secret* (p xii). Scottsdale, AZ: Bridge of Love Publications USA.
[46] Ibid, pp xii-xiii.

the same time, creating institutions like religions to mentally and emotionally imprison the masses and set them at war with each other." [47]

Clearly, this present magnitude of planetary control did not take place within a few years, but has been thousands of years in the making.

All institutions are affected: government, banking, business, military and media; and, in actual fact, have not been infiltrated by the Brotherhood, given that they were first and foremost created by the Brotherhood; hence the "Brotherhood Agenda is, in truth, the Agenda of many Millennia. It is the unfolding of a plan, piece by piece, for the centralised control of the planet." [48]

The bloodline hierarchy that resides at the top of the pyramid basically represents the 5% that are controlling us, the multitude, the remaining 95%.

"The children of these family lines who are chosen to inherit the baton are brought up from birth to understand the Agenda and the methods of manipulating the 'Great Work' into reality. Advancing the Agenda becomes their

---

[47] Icke, David. (1999). *The Biggest Secret* (p 1). Scottsdale, AZ: Bridge of Love Publications USA.
[48] Ibid, p 2.

indoctrinated mission from very early in their lives. By the time their turn comes to join the Brotherhood hierarchy and carry the baton into the next generation, their upbringing has molded them into highly imbalanced people. They are intellectually very sharp, but with a compassion bypass and an arrogance that they have the right to rule the world and control the ignorant masses who they view as inferior. Any Brotherhood children who threaten to challenge or reject that mold are pushed aside or dealt with in other ways to ensure that only 'safe' people make it to the upper levels of the pyramid and the highly secret and advanced knowledge that is held there." [49]

Icke believes that the starting point of this manipulation goes back hundreds of thousands of years to a race (or races) from other dimensions of evolution.

As plausible as this may be, given that we are not alone in this vast universe, I have not done any research into the possible authenticity of such a claim.

However, this does not retract, in any way, from his overall message.

---

[49] Icke, David. (1999). *The Biggest Secret* (p 2). Scottsdale, AZ: Bridge of Love Publications USA.

Icke speaks of the lower fourth dimension as being the dimension whereby control and manipulation is primarily orchestrated. He mentions the Annunaki of ancient Sumeria, courtesy of Zecharia Sitchin, claiming that the Brotherhood bloodline is traceable to the Annunaki extraterrestrials who were revered as 'gods'.

American researcher, David Sielaff, emphasises that "the Nefilim or Nephilim are not the sons of the gods, but the offspring of the interbreeding between the "daughters of men" and the non-humans the Bible calls the Elohim meaning that the Iluminati bloodlines that rule the world today are the Nefilim, a race of human/non-human hybrids. They were also known in ancient times as the Rephaim, Emim, Zazummin and Anakim, and they were all very tall or 'giant' people in those days." [50]

Could this mating have resulted in the origin of the divine right of kings, meaning the right to rule by virtue of family bloodline, a system which appears to have continued into the present day?

----

[50] Icke, David. (2003). *Tales from The Time Loop* (p 231). Wildwood, MO: Bridge of Love Publications USA.

Even more interesting is the fact that, according to Icke, the most important gene in such a bloodline succession appears to be passed on by the *female*.

This takes us back to the pharaonic tradition of brothers marrying their sisters or half-sisters. This Egyptian royal line, said to be most important to the Illuminati, has survived intact to the modern era.

Whether they be reptilian, shape-shifting, beings or not, there *has* been a perpetuation of a specific bloodline, the Babylonian Brotherhood of which Icke speaks.

"This 'Divine' right to rule has nothing to do with the 'Divine' and everything to do with the real origin of these bloodlines. They claim to descend from the 'gods' of the ancient world. The 'royal' families have interbred incessantly with each other since ancient times because they are seeking to retain the DNA corruption that can apparently be quickly diluted by breeding outside of itself." [51]

In accordance with Icke's theory, the bloodlines of European royalty evolved from this same bloodline while "the crown evolved from the horned headgear worn by Nimrod. The

---

[51] Icke, David. (2003). *Tales from The Time Loop* (p 38). Wildwood, MO: Bridge of Love Publications USA.

31

horns symbolised the monarch's authority and later became a metal headband with three horns symbolising royal power with divine authority. This is represented by the symbol of the fleur-de-lis which you find throughout the regalia of modern royalty." [52]

According to Icke, all genetic links back to Charlemagne are of the Illuminati bloodline.

"The royal 'Divine' bloodlines of ancient Sumer and Babylon (now Iraq), Egypt, the Indus Valley and elsewhere expanded into Europe to become the royal and aristocratic families that rules the continent and most of the word through the British Empire and those of France, Belgium, the Netherlands, Germany and so on. As the people began to challenge and reject the open dictatorship of royal rule the bloodlines began to move 'underground' by operating among the population in all of the areas that control modern society." [53]

Wherever they went, "the Babylonian Brotherhood created their own mystery schools to manipulate the population into believing nonsense and into giving away their power

---

[52] Icke, David. (1999). *The Biggest Secret* (p 51). Scottsdale, AZ: Bridge of Love Publications USA.

[53] Icke, David. (2003). *Tales from The Time Loop* (p 38). Wildwood, MO: Bridge of Love Publications USA.

through superstition and fear. Where other non-reptilian initiation schools existed, they were infiltrated and taken over by the Babylonian priesthood." [54]

Icke also makes mention of the Jesuits, the secret society that controls the Catholic Church, as being one of the most powerful expressions of the Illuminati to this day.

"Official history has been changed to hide the fact that the world has been controlled by the same interbreeding tribe for thousands of years. This is never more so than with the major religions. They all have inner and outer levels of knowing. The inner level carries the secrets going back to the ancient mystery schools of places like Sumer, Babylon and Egypt. These include the secrets of the bloodline and only the chosen few are initiated into this awareness. The outer level is where the secrets are hidden in code and allegory and sold, with a deity, to the masses as the 'truth'. The New Testament Gospel stories are based on the initiation ceremonies and esoteric secrets, including astrology and Sun worship, that were performed and communicated in the mystery schools. But they are represented as a literal story to fool the people. The

---

[54] Icke, David. (1999). *The Biggest Secret* (p 56). Scottsdale, AZ: Bridge of Love Publications USA.

religions, not least Christianity, Judaism and Islam (all spawned from the same source) are carriers of the secrets (inner) and controllers of the people by hiding the secrets with allegedly 'literal' stories (outer)." [55]

"The same basic 'Jesus' tale of the Son of God who dies for humanity was told around the world thousands of years before Christianity. This is related to the winter solstice or midwinter festival when the Sun is at the least powerful point in its cycle in the northern hemisphere. They said that on the solstice, our December 21/ 22, the Sun had 'died'. Three days later – the 25TH – they said the Sun was born or born again. Thus we have a long line of Sun gods given the 'birthday' of December 25. The Jesus of the Gospels is a symbol of the Sun and the stories include a host of other mystery school knowledge and esoteric concepts." [56]

Knowing that in ancient times Sumer and Babylon (now Iraq) were both headquarters for the Illuminati, Icke shares that "it was the accounts, texts and artefacts ... that were burned and looted from Iraqi museums in the wake of the American and British invasion. After Babylon, the Illuminati

---

[55] Icke, David. (2003). *Tales from The Time Loop* (p 41). Wildwood, MO: Bridge of Love Publications USA.

[56] Ibid.

bloodline network moved its headquarters to Rome and it was during this time that we had the Roman Empire and the creation of the Roman Church or institutionalised Christianity. The Roman Catholic Church structure controlled by the Jesuit secret society remains at the heart of Illuminati operations." [57]

After the fall of the Roman Empire, "operational headquarters moved into northern Europe ... for a period of time ... based in Amsterdam" [58] during the time when the Dutch East India Company became prominent, settling in South Africa. "In 1688, William of Orange, one of the bloodlines, invaded England from the Netherlands and took the throne as William III in 1689." [59] We have now come full circle to present day headquarters.

"When the European empires began to recede and collapse, especially in the twentieth century, it appeared that ... colony continents, like the Americas, Africa, Asia and Australia, had won their 'independence'. Instead, the Illuminati bloodlines were merely exchanging open control for the far more effective covert control", thereby leading to a

[57] Icke, David. (2003). *Tales from The Time Loop* (p 41). Wildwood, MO: Bridge of Love Publications USA.
[58] Ibid, pp 43-44.
[59] Ibid, p 44.

"manipulation of events by the Hidden Hand that the public has no idea exists." [60]

I agree wholeheartedly with Icke when he says that "there should be no structures, whatever their intent, that deny knowledge to people" [61] and "once you consider it your right to deny knowledge and decide who should and who should not have access to it, you are playing a very dangerous and arrogant game" [62] for this is what has allowed the coordination and perpetuation of the Brotherhood Agenda.

It is also my belief that there were "those of positive intent who wanted to use the mystery schools to give the knowledge to people they believed would use it wisely." [63]

"Knowledge is not good nor bad; it just is. It is how we use that knowledge that is positive or negative. At the upper levels of this network they know of the true power of the Sun, magnetics and the mind; the effect of the planets on human behavior; how to manipulate time, consciousness,

---

[60] Icke, David. (2003). *Tales from The Time Loop* (p 44). Wildwood, MO: Bridge of Love Publications USA.
[61] Icke, David. (1999). *The Biggest Secret* (pp 56-57). Scottsdale, AZ: Bridge of Love Publications USA.
[62] Ibid, p 57.
[63] Ibid.

energy, the weather and so much more. If used malevolently, this knowledge can be incredibly destructive and manipulating and this is what has happened." [64]

In essence, "the Brotherhood priests and initiates would hijack the positions of religious and political power and ensure that any advanced knowledge in circulation was sucked out of the public domain and into their mystery schools and secret societies." [65]

Apparently the British Isles are an extremely sacred place to the Brotherhood, mainly due to the Isles being equated with the center of the Earth's energy grid. It was for this very reason that the Brotherhood made their way to Britain, establishing their headquarters in London where it has remained to this day.

Icke makes an interesting comparison to there being "a greater concentration of stone circles, standing stones, ancient mounds and sites, in areas of Britain than in almost anywhere else in the world." [66]

---

[64] Icke, David. (1999). *The Biggest Secret* (p 57). Scottsdale, AZ: Bridge of Love Publications USA.
[65] Ibid, p 58.
[66] Ibid, p 74.

This Babylonian Brotherhood hierarchy focused on the Sun because "they understood the true nature of the Sun as a multidimensional consciousness which extends across the solar system on unseen frequency levels." [67] In addition, "they understood its true power as an amazing generator of electromagnetic energy." [68]

Can you imagine "the power you would have to advance an Agenda and manipulate the human race if you knew the cycles of energy from the Sun and other planets and how they were likely to effect human consciousness. You would know when people would be more prone to anger, aggression, fear, doubt and guilt, and therefore when to have your wars, economic collapses and so on." [69]

According to Icke, the Brotherhood have always had this knowledge and they use it to great effect, even today.

In addition, the Brotherhood have always had "enormous knowledge of the Earth's energy grid and its potential to affect human consciousness. After all, we live within the planet's magnetic field. When it changes, we change. If you live in water and the water changes, you are fundamentally

---

[67] Icke, David. (1999). *The Biggest Secret* (p 55). Scottsdale, AZ: Bridge of Love Publications USA.
[68] Ibid, p 78.
[69] Ibid, p 56.

affected and it is the same with the energy 'ocean' that we occupy. Thus you have the movement of the planets affecting the Earth's magnetic field and through that affecting us." [70]

According to Icke, the "bloodlines, the 'chosen people' of the gods, and the secret knowledge, are symbolised as 'the vine' and 'vineyards' in the Bible and countless other writings and pictures." [71]

However, he does not believe that this bloodline is suggestive in any way of the bloodline of King David, saying that he did not exist.

Instead, the royal blood, or Sang Raal, the old French term, was meant to identify none other than the "bloodlines of the reptilian-human crossbreeds." [72]

Instead, the "symbolism of the vine can ... be traced back to Babylon and Egypt ... weaved in among the Sun symbolism that is one of the royal and priestly bloodlines which lead back to the reptilians, the Annunaki," [73] so much so that as

---

[70] Icke, David. (1999). *The Biggest Secret* (p 66). Scottsdale, AZ: Bridge of Love Publications USA.
[71] Ibid, p 98.
[72] Ibid, p 107.
[73] Ibid, p 98.

the years passed, "the Sun religion and the esoteric symbolism of the mystery schools, were transformed into a religion based on a literal translation of symbolic texts." [74]

It can be said that it was "on this misunderstanding and deceit, Christianity was built." [75]

All of the world's major religions, Hinduism, Christianity, Judaism and Islam, are said to have come out of the same region. "These religions were designed to imprison the mind and engulf the emotions with fear and guilt," [76] based on a savior-like figure in whom one had to believe, thereby following their dictates.

In fact, there was a Jerome born in 341, who has been credited with "wanting the priests to be the middle men between humanity and God. He did not want people going direct, contradicting the official line, or circulating unapproved knowledge." [77]

Clearly "Constantine, and the Brotherhood which controlled the emperors, saw political advantage in supporting the

---

[74] Icke, David. (1999). *The Biggest Secret* (p 109). Scottsdale, AZ: Bridge of Love Publications USA.
[75] Ibid.
[76] Ibid, p 78.
[77] Ibid, p 112.

Christian movement. And the people would have no problem encompassing Jesus into their belief system because the story matched that of the other Sun gods of the time, including Mithra." [78]

One has to wonder about a religion that has "persecuted, burned and tortured anyone who refused in the Christian faith, or even their version of the faith. Tens of millions of people have died in the name of the so-called *Prince of Peace*." [79]

Reflecting back on the horrors of the Inquisition and the Albigensian Crusades with regards to the Cathars, to cite just two examples, is enough to give one food for thought.

Christianity, like Judaism and Islam, was "designed to achieve another vital part of the reptilian Agenda: the suppression of the female energy, the intuitive connection to higher levels of our multidimensional consciousness. Once you suppress your feminine energy, your intuition, you switch off your higher consciousness and become dominated by your lower consciousness. You are isolated from your highest expression of love, wisdom and knowledge, and at

---

[78] Icke, David. (1999). *The Biggest Secret* (p 110). Scottsdale, AZ: Bridge of Love Publications USA.
[79] Ibid, p 111.

the mercy of the manipulated 'information' bombarding your eyes and ears. This is why the Brotherhood have sought to create a world in which the male energy has called the shots." [80]

In short, Christianity was "a male bastion from its very foundation, created to suppress the balancing female energy." [81]

In keeping, the Christian Church "was built to represent and perpetuate the extreme male vibration, the Sun energy, and to keep the ancient knowledge secret. The Christian Church became a crucial and highly effective vehicle to remove knowledge from circulation so it could be used secretly and malevolently behind the scenes. The assault on the balancing female energy and the hoarding of knowledge resulted in the persecution of 'witches' – channellers, mediums, psychics and seers of all kinds." [82]

And yet these initiates of the Babylonian Brotherhood, these creators of the Roman Church, were "using these same

---

[80] Icke, David. (1999). *The Biggest Secret* (p 111). Scottsdale, AZ: Bridge of Love Publications USA.
[81] Ibid, p 112.
[82] Ibid.

psychic   powers   and   modes   on   inter-dimensional communication." [83]

No doubt about it. Whether extraterrestrials or not, we have been manipulated and controlled in an overwhelmingly monumental and mind boggling way.

Today, the "initiates and frontmen for the Babylonian Brotherhood control world politics, banking, business, intelligence agencies, police, the military, education and the media. The most important of these, in terms of control, is banking," [84] as alluded to earlier. Such is a means of systematic manipulation in order to steal the real wealth of the world.

However, "the control and manipulation of the media and other institutions which direct human thinking and perception is not only to achieve power for power's sake, there is a much bigger reason for it. The Agenda is for the complete takeover of the planet ... without anyone realising that it has even happened." [85]

---

[83] Icke, David. (1999). *The Biggest Secret* (p 113). Scottsdale, AZ: Bridge of Love Publications USA.
[84] Ibid, p 207.
[85] Ibid, p 273.

"The basic structure is designed around a world government which would make all the major decisions in the world. This would control a world central bank, currency (electronic, no cash), and army. All this would be underpinned by a microchipped population linked to a global computer. Under this structure would come three superstates: The European Union, the American Union and the Pacific Union (Asia, Far East, Australia). This edifice of power would dictate to the current nation states which are planned to be broken up into regions to dismantle any unified response." [86]

Beneath all, would lie the people. Unless we awaken from our slumber, we are facing a global fascist dictatorship, if, indeed, we are not there already.

As a means of furthering this agenda, "one of the most powerful weapons in the Brotherhood's war against humanity ... has been addictive and mind-altering drugs. In the ancient mystery schools, drugs were widely employed to stimulate other states of consciousness and to manipulate thought and perception." [87]

---

[86] Icke, David. (1999). *The Biggest Secret* (p 274). Scottsdale, AZ: Bridge of Love Publications USA.
[87] Ibid, p 280.

"The drug trade is not only about making vast amounts of money, although that is important to fund the Agenda into place, it is also designed to break down societies and stop young people manifesting their true worth and potential. When people are hooked on drugs they are not going to be a problem to the Brotherhood's grand design." [88]

As I stated before, when you control a person's mind you control the person. "The external manipulation of the mind takes many forms and the question is not how many are mind controlled, but how few are not. Every time you allow a newspaper, news program or manipulating advertisement to affect your perceptions and decisions, you are being mind controlled." [89]

"Most people find it impossible to accept that a few people can manipulate the lives of billions and operate through all institutions and countries." [90]

"When a few people wish to control and direct a mass of humanity, there are certain structures that have to be in place. First you have to impose the 'norm', what are

––––––––––––––

[88] Icke, David. (1999). *The Biggest Secret* (p 285). Scottsdale, AZ: Bridge of Love Publications USA.
[89] Ibid, p 312.
[90] Icke, David. (2003). *Tales from The Time Loop* (p 47). Wildwood, MO: Bridge of Love Publications USA.

considered right and wrong, possible or impossible, sane or insane, good or bad. Most of the people will follow those 'norms' without question because of the baa-baa, herd mentality that has prevailed within the collective human mind for ... thousands of years. Second, you have to make life very unpleasant for those few who challenge your imposed 'norms'. The 'norms' or 'consensus reality', are essential to our control" [91] (meaning control of the masses).

"The most effective way to do this in order to ensure compliance with these norms, is to make it difficult to be different. You make those who voice a different view, version of 'truth' and lifestyle, stand out like a black sheep in the human herd. You have already conditioned the herd to accept your norms as its reality and, through arrogance and ignorance, they ridicule or condemn those with a different spin on life. This pressurises the black sheep to conform and serves as a warning to those others in the herd who are also thinking of breaking away or challenging the prevailing reality." [92]

"This mentality means that the masses are policing themselves and keeping each other in line. The sheep

---

[91] Icke, David. (2003). *Tales from The Time Loop* (p 47). Wildwood, MO: Bridge of Love Publications USA.
[92] Ibid.

become the sheepdog for the rest of the herd. This is nothing less than psychological fascism: the Thought Police with agents in every home ... "I'm just doing what's right for my children" ... No, what you have been programmed to believe is right for them and the belief, also, that only you know best." [93]

"This is all part of the divide and rule strategy so vital to the few controlling the many. Everyone plays a part in everyone else's mental, emotional and physical imprisonment. All the controllers have to do is set the 'norms', pull the right strings at the right time and make their human puppets dance to the appropriate tune. This they do by dictating what is taught in what we bravely call 'education' and controlling what passes for 'news' through the Illuminati owned media. In this way they can dictate to the unthinking, unquestioning herd what it should believe about itself, other people, life, history and current events. Once you set the 'norms' there is no need to control every journalist or reporter or government official. The media and the institutions take their 'truth' from those same 'norms' and official statements, and

[93] Icke, David. (2003). *Tales from The Time Loop* (p 95). Wildwood, MO: Bridge of Love Publications USA.

ridicule and condemn by reflex action anyone who offers another vision of reality." [94]

"The self-policing of the human herd ... starts with conditioned parents who impose their conditioning on their children and pressure them to follow their religious, political, economic and cultural norms." [95]

"Once you have the herd mentality policing itself, there is a third phase in this entrapment of human consciousness. You create factions within the herd and set them to war with each other. This is done by creating 'different' belief systems (which are not different at all) and bring them into conflict. These belief systems are known as religions, political parties, economic theories and "isms" of an endless variety." [96]

"There are techniques of mass manipulation that people need to understand if they are to begin to see through the game. Problem – Reaction – Solution is one that has been

---

[94] Icke, David. (2003). *Tales from The Time Loop* (p 48). Wildwood, MO: Bridge of Love Publications USA.
[95] Ibid.
[96] Ibid, p 48.

used for thousands of years to advance the agenda and is one of the most effective weapons of the Illuminati." [97]

The Problem – Reaction – Solution agenda works in the following manner.

"You know that if you openly propose to remove basic freedoms, start a war on centralise power, there will be a public reaction against it. So you don't openly and honestly propose such plans, you play the Problem – Reaction – Solution scam. At stage one you <u>create a problem</u>. It could be a country attacking another, a government or economic collapse, or a 'terrorist attack'. Anything in fact that the public will think requires a 'solution'. At stage two, you <u>report the problems</u> you have covertly created in the way you wish people to perceive them. Crucially you find someone to blame for the problem. You spin the background to these events in a way that encourages the people to demand that "something must be done". These are the words you want to hear because they allow you to move on to stage three, the sting. At this point you <u>openly offer the solutions to the problems</u> you have yourself created. These solutions, of course, involve the centralisation of power, the seeking of officials or politicians that are getting in your way, and the

---

[97] Icke, David. (2003). *Tales from The Time Loop* (p 49). Wildwood, MO: Bridge of Love Publications USA.

removal of more basic freedoms as you advance further to your global fascist state." [98]

With this very technique, "you can so manipulate the public mind that people will demand or at least allow you to introduce what, in normal circumstances, they would vehemently oppose." [99]

Can you not see how they are going about their business?

"First they were the royalty and nobility of the ancients and now they are the leading politicians, bankers, businessmen and media owners of modern society." [100]

I was first introduced to Cathy O' Brien through my research and reading material as published by both Ivan Fraser and David Icke. This lead to my locating an online video, filmed at the Granada Forum in 1996.

In her book, *Trance-Formation of America*, Cathy has written about a little known tool that the United States Government is covertly, illegally, and unconstitutionally

------

[98] Icke, David. (2003). *Tales from The Time Loop* (pp 49-50). Wildwood, MO: Bridge of Love Publications USA.
[99] Ibid, p 50.
[100] Ibid, p 230.

using to implement the New World Order (also known as One World Government).

This well documented tool is a sophisticated and advanced form of behavior modification (brainwashing) known as MIND CONTROL.

Hitler was particularly interested in mind control, knowing that people who are abused become extremely receptive to external control of their mind. In keeping, he assigned his right-hand man, Heinrich Himmler, to do research on individuals of "Northern European multi-generation sexually abused, psychologically abused and physically abused children." [101]

Multi-generational abuse begins at birth, as was also the case for O'Brien. She became an MK-Ultra mind control slave; the exact project that Hitler first assigned to Himmler.

Mark Phillips, a former Department of Defense (DOD) sub-contractor whose skills were utilized in the area of subliminal marketing, became a subliminal persuasion expert. Due to the fact that he could keep a secret, he was given Defense Department clearance.

---

[101] 1996 Granada Forum Video, accessed on June 29, 2006, located at http://video.google.com/videoplay?docid=-292771133640787454

Phillips knew about the Heinrich Himmler studies for Adolf Hitler.

He knew that "Adolph Hitler wanted to develop some very serious people to put in places to control various regions in what he called, and what George Bush called, and Nero called, the NEW WORLD ORDER. Adolf Hitler was not the first, nor was George Bush, to fantasize about this hideous idea of totalitarian government, thereby enslaving the entire globe through mind-manipulation." [102]

The surreal part to all of this is that the information that Hitler was developing was perpetuated in the United States by way of Project Paperclip, "the importation of Nazi and fascist scientists into the country after World War II." [103]

In O'Brien's book it is shared that when slaves have outlived their usefulness and/or their programming begins to break down, they are murdered. It is a rarity that they are allowed to live beyond their 30th birthday.

Is it possible that Hitler's version of world domination is currently being implemented?

---

[102] 1996 Granada Forum Video, accessed on June 29, 2006, located at http://video.google.com/videoplay?docid=-292771133640787454

[103] Ibid.

Under MK-Ultra (Project Monarch) trauma-based mind control, O'Brien lost complete and total control over her own free will, unable to question, unable to reason, unable to consciously comprehend what was happening, responding only as programmed from a robotic level.

O'Brien was so powerfully mind controlled that she was 'promoted' to become what she terms a Presidential Model, meaning a mind controlled slave who is detailed to operate with the top people in the White House and the Pentagon.

In *Trance-Formation of America*, O'Brien actually names individuals, all shown to be pedophiles, modern-day vampires, Satanists and murderers, but with different roles to play.

In essence, she had been programmed to be a high class prostitute for select politicians, taught how to gratify any sexual perversion.

What does this have to do with the New World Order, you ask?

The involvement of the United States "in drug distribution, pornography, and white slavery was *justified* as a means of gaining control of all illegal activities worldwide to fund

Black Budget covert activity that would bring world peace through world dominance and mind control." [104]

In addition, there were many who "adhered to the belief that 95% of the (world's) people *want* to be led by the 5% because the 95% *do not want to know* what really goes on in government." [105]

As alarming as this may sound, this validates that which was put forth earlier.

The Director of Project Monarch slaves, a former U.S. President, is quoted as saying that he "did not perceive mind control as slavery, but as an opportunity for those who otherwise would have nothing in life." [106]

Additional words attributed to this Director were that "order must come first because without it, law would be ineffective. Sometimes we must rise above and beyond the law to establish that order – or a new (world) order. Establish

---

[104] O'Brien, Cathy and Phillips, Mark. (1995). *Trance-Formation of America* (p 119). Guntersville, AB: Reality Marketing, Incorporated.
[105] Ibid.
[106] Ibid, p 126.

order through democracy by spreading democracy throughout the world. With order, there is peace." [107]

Having read the words penned by Cathy O'Brien, I can honestly say that this view of democracy does not, in any way, shape or form, mesh with my own.

True democracy is one where all persons have a voice and are recognized as being important.

In keeping, true democracy would not allow for a wide variety of smuggling across both the Canadian border as well as the Mexican border – illegal business activity, the trafficking of drugs as well as mind-controlled slaves (be they children or adults).

In sharing from her perspective, O'Brien states that "those who were actively laying the groundwork for implementing the New World Order through mind conditioning of the masses made no distinction between Democratic and Republican parties." [108]

---

[107] O'Brien, Cathy and Phillips, Mark. (1995). *Trance-Formation of America* (p 145). Guntersville, AB: Reality Marketing, Incorporated.
[108] Ibid, p 152.

In keeping with the signing of the North American Free Trade Agreement (NAFTA), it is O'Brien's understanding that this "was considered a significant step in implementing the New World Order through mind manipulation of the masses." [109]

One needs to look no father than Education 2000, as per the United States, "designed to increase our children's learning capacity while destroying their ability to critically think for themselves." [110]

I personally find this rather terrifying, given the propensity that Canada has for following the educational trends as set by the United States.

Although the vast majority is not being mind-manipulated to the extreme degree as has been O'Brien's experience, rest assured, we are being manipulated by the Illuminati controlled media. As a world-wide people, it has become imperative that we know that our minds, our religions and our perceptions are being *deliberately* manipulated by the 5% maintaining control.

---

[109] O'Brien, Cathy and Phillips, Mark. (1995). *Trance-Formation of America* (p 160). Guntersville, AB: Reality Marketing, Incorporated.
[110] Ibid, p 175.

O'Brien shares further in saying "I know for a fact that the plan is to make all of us feel totally helpless; that what's happening is beyond our realm to affect because we've been taken over by aliens, that our Independence Day is dawning. So beware of that." [111]

Most unfortunately, "superstition begins where knowledge leaves off. And they have been keeping knowledge from us for a long time. People have all kinds of belief systems and I'm sure each one of you has various and different belief systems as well. Regardless of what your belief system is, it is imperative that you know that these criminals are people" meaning that "they *are* within our realm to affect." [112]

O'Brien firmly believes that "there can be no world peace without peace-of-mind, and there is no peace-of-mind under mind control." [113]

"The ramifications of mind-control are far-reaching. I also know that under mind-control there's no free thought. Without free thought there's no free will. Without God-given free will there's no soul expression. What kind of

---

[111] O'Brien, Cathy and Phillips, Mark. (1995). *Trance-Formation of America* (p 175). Guntersville, AB: Reality Marketing, Incorporated.
[112] Ibid.
[113] Ibid, p 192.

a world peace can we have without any free will or soul expression, without any spirituality? Mind-control needs to be exposed in order that people maintain their freedom of thought. In order that people maintain their free will, and have that spiritual expression. Because when people have soul and spirituality, they're going to be acting in a capacity of love anyway. That is where world peace is! Not in mind-control." [114]

When we "are under the spell of fear we delink ourselves from our true connection to infinity and live our lives within a small droplet of consciousness, the egg shell. When we express the emotion of love we reconnect with our multidimensional self and our potential becomes infinite because we become infinite. We reconnect with the ocean, with God." [115] In reconnecting, we feel a deep sense of balance, a deep sense of inner harmony.

It is also important to remember that what we give out (thought forms, feelings and emotions) is what we get back.

_____

[114] 1996 Granada Forum Video, accessed on June 29, 2006, located at http://video.google.com/videoplay?docid=-292771133640787454

[115] Icke, David. (1999). *The Biggest Secret* (p 467). Scottsdale, AZ: Bridge of Love Publications USA.

Everything resonates at a frequency. A symbol, being a physical representation of a thought, therefore becomes a powerful example of what we can work with, be it for the good or the bad.

"Fear of something is always guaranteed to attract what you fear. The energy of fear attracts like energy and what you fear becomes what you physically experience." [116]

We create by way of our own thoughts and feelings. In association with the Brotherhood Agenda, we can say that we have allowed our thoughts and feelings to be manipulated by religion, politics, education, science, etc.

Upon this realization, this manipulation is not a bad thing, because it means that "if you created the present reality that you don't like, you can just as easily create a new reality that you do. You are in control. You have all the answers. You are the centre of your own universe and you can make it whatever you choose. You are simply incredible. Feel it, live it and your world will be transformed." [117]

---

[116] Icke, David. (1999). *The Biggest Secret* (p 448). Scottsdale, AZ: Bridge of Love Publications USA.
[117] Ibid, p 488.

"The Illuminati seek to construct a 'consensus reality' in which the collective human mind, Jung's collective unconscious, accepts the prevailing 'truth' it is programmed to believe." [118]

"On this planet alone the best part of six billion people resonate to the illusions of the Matrix and that is why the Matrix can continue. We cannot bring the Matrix prison to a conclusion by reacting 'out there' with guns, bombs, anger and hatred because that will make the Matrix frequency even stronger by adding to its patterns of disharmony. The answer lies 'in here' as we change our own frequency patterns and connect with Oneness, harmony and love. If we change ourselves, we change our 'world', our reality. Only then will the Matrix pattern be overwhelmed by a mass vibrational change that will undermine the stability of the frequency fields that hold its imprisoned minds in such servitude to the 'material' illusion." [119]

As long as one is controlled by rigid dogma and a closed mind, the Matrix has you.

---

[118] Icke, David. (2003). *Tales from The Time Loop* (p 362). Wildwood, MO: Bridge of Love Publications USA.
[119] Ibid, pp 363-364.

Most believe that we are human beings having a spiritual experience. In flip-flopping this statement, we become spiritual beings having a human experience which is consistent with my belief.

As we continue to awaken, we will start to realize, and want to work with, our true potential. We will "help to heal and awaken humanity; learn how to expand and evolve our minds in harmony with the universe; live in peace with all life forms, many of whom we are still to acknowledge and meet." [120]

Hyde further shares that he is "convinced that Jesus, Buddha and Shri Krishna lived amongst us to teach us how to heal our lives and evolve, as examples of love, sensitivity, compassion and forgiveness. Unfortunately, certain individuals throughout most of our history have kept the real truths from us. The Bible, it would be fair to say, has had some very significant truths deleted and insignificant texts added such that it is now far removed from Jesus' original teachings." [121]

---

[120] Hyde, Mark. "UFOs – A Brief History". The Truth Campaign magazine. December 1996: Volume 3, page 20.
[121] Ibid.

One merely has to research the Council of Nicaea to develop an insight into the orthodox (correct theological observance as determined by some overseeing body) ideas that arose during this creation of the early Roman Church.

"Consciousness in its reconnected infinite power could easily take control, but it is difficult to do this when you are not aware that you are Infinite Consciousness. The aim is to turn conscious beings into generators of fear in all its forms to empower the Matrix, and to take away freedom and replace it with what I call feardom, meaning domination by fear." [122]

To sum it up simply, fear = control = power for the Matrix.

As Icke shares further, "if you are awake enough to reject conventional religion, the Matrix has other options. You can worship the gods of money, 'status', and power over others. These obsessions are religions under other names and also dictate what you must do, think and say to achieve your goal." [123]

---

[122] Icke, David. (2005). *Infinite Love is the Only Truth - Everything Else is Illusion* (p 81). Wildwood, MO: Bridge of Love Publications USA.
[123] Ibid, pp 130-131.

However, "the further you move yourself from the collective norms the more you remove the chains of collective reality and the Matrix." [124] How does one, therefore, go about reclaiming their power in order to think anew for themselves? Icke makes note of steps with which to begin.

"Step One – Refuse to have another tell you what to think and do with your life. What matters is that you are you and not what someone else is telling you to be. Respect the freedom of others to do the same.

"Step Two – As the process of unplugging continues, things that mattered to you before become less important and your outlook on life and others starts to transform. You become more tolerant of yourself and others. Your attitudes to everything change once the recognition of the illusion goes deeper and deeper and you start to be that awareness rather than just intellectually accepting its existence. Don't think it, know it. Don't try to do it, just do it. These are very different states of being. When you become more consciously aware of the illusion, you can begin to enjoy it without all the hang-ups that imprison us when we think it is real. We can have fun and express our desires, as long as they don't impinge on the freedom of others.

---

[124] Icke, David. (2003). *Tales from The Time Loop* (p 442). Wildwood, MO: Bridge of Love Publications USA.

"Step Three – Taking ... responsibility and ceasing to blame others – or ourselves come to that – is to take a massive step on the freedom road. The power the Illuminati use to control and manipulate is only the power we give away to them and others every day. The most destructive expression of this is blaming others for our plight. In truth, only we have that power if we choose to use it; but if we believe that others are in control of our destiny we will create that reality.

"Step Four – We need to start focusing on the right to freedom of expression" [125] for all. This can also be translated to treating all persons with respect.

If we believe that division and separateness exists, the Matrix has us for it promotes this duality.

Oneness = Love = Balance

Hatred = Illusion of Division = Disharmony

"Once you realize that your programmed reactions are not *you* there will be far more harmony and peace in your life. There are still moments when the program will con you into reacting, but the more you express consciousness the less

---

[125] Icke, David. (2003). *Tales from The Time Loop* (pp 445-448). Wildwood, MO: Bridge of Love Publications USA.

this will happen and the quicker you will apply the brake when it does." [126]

In addition, "we don't need to learn, we need to *un*learn what the program has manipulated us to believe. Mind is not the road to enlightenment; it is the *barrier* to it. Knowledge and *knowing* is not the same thing – one is mind, the other consciousness. We don't need to learn, but to awaken from the hypnotic trance and remember who we are. When we do, we cease to *think* and start to *know*. Some call this intuition or following the heart." [127]

What Icke shares next can be just a tad confusing, but completely relevant to coming back to oneself.

"To truly connect in awareness with the One, we need to stop making choices, stop trying to change anything and have no sense of purpose. To be without purpose does not mean to sit down and do nothing; it is to cease to identify who you are with what you are doing and no longer let what

---

[126] Icke, David. (2005). *Infinite Love is the Only Truth - Everything Else is Illusion* (p 185). Wildwood, MO: Bridge of Love Publications USA.
[127] Ibid, p 187.

you do define you. What you do just *is* instead of what you *are*." [128]

It gets just a wee bit more integral in this next segment.

"If we don't pursue purpose, choice and change, does that mean we just sit around and do nothing while the Illuminati impose terror, control and mayhem? Well, yes and no. It is not about *doing*, but *being*. To *do* is to make a choice to do. It is a process of thought and that is the program, the Matrix, creating polarities. To *be* is to *know* – the One. The pursuit of purpose and *doing* gets in the way of that." [129]

"Oneness is the balance of all, and the Illuminati agenda is not balance, but polarities. To challenge the Illuminati is not balance, but polarity. To *be* is to encompass them *both* and identify with *neither*." [130]

"When we come from the perspective of Oneness and move with the flow of knowingness, things just happen without us needing to choose, think, fight or pursue." [131]

---

[128] Icke, David. (2005). *Infinite Love is the Only Truth - Everything Else is Illusion* (pp 191-192). Wildwood, MO: Bridge of Love Publications USA.
[129] Ibid, p 193.
[130] Ibid.
[131] Ibid.

In essence, therefore, "the road to freedom and Oneness is not to create polarities, but to encompass them." [132]

If we want change for the better, "we need to understand first what we have to deal with, and secondly that real change will not come from the top down, but rather from the bottom up" [133] which clearly means that, in order to be in control of our own lives, we must also take responsibility for ourselves. Collectively, all are responsible for the current state of affairs.

"For meaningful changes to take place ... it begins in the hearts and minds of individuals who look around and see things for what they are." [134]

Am I, as an individual, where Icke claims I need to be in reference to simply being?

Not yet, but I am doing my best to disengage from the Matrix in a manner that befits me at the present time, courtesy of the following steps.

---

[132] Icke, David. (2005). *Infinite Love is the Only Truth - Everything Else is Illusion* (pp 191-192). Wildwood, MO: Bridge of Love Publications USA.
[133] Greaves, Richard. "Who Runs the World?". The Truth Campaign magazine. Autumn 2001: Issue 22, p 26.
[134] Ibid, p 27.

(1) Total detachment from the media.

I no longer watch the news on TV. I have stopped reading the newspapers. I do not listen to the news on the radio. I have stopped reading news related magazines.

This was the first step for me in releasing myself from the fear and negativity that abounds within the Brotherhood controlled media.

As a result of my Masters program, I came to better understand that TV stations report what they are told to report, namely, biased media events which serve to perpetuate the imbalance that exists.

Once awareness has been heightened to the degree that the viewer can think of nothing else, focusing and channeling their energies on the negative events (these seem to be the ones portrayed), such continues to perpetuate the divide, rule and conquer mentality which feeds on unstable emotions.

(2) Seeking the truth.

I am learning to detach from what I have been manipulated into believing, because therein lies the containment, the imprisonment.

I am also learning to challenge.

I am learning to seek truth in whatever form resonates within my very soul, within my very consciousness.

I am starting to remember who I am.

(3) Becoming the change I wish to see in the world.

I am letting go of fear, refusing to give it power.

I am placing an increased focus on the positive so as to generate more of this vibration.

I am endeavoring to connect with my highest level of wisdom.

I am allowing love and inspiration to guide what I deem most appropriate for myself.

I am becoming peace.

I am becoming forgiveness.

I believe in doing unto others as I would have them do unto me.

I am celebrating diversity.

I am demonstrating compassion.

I am meditating and surrendering to the stillness.

I am listening to my intuitive heart.

Truly, it is all about being brave enough to transform your very being.

(4) Continuing to focus on the good and the positive.

There are exciting, wonderful and beautiful things happening on the planet, many of which are extremely promising.

"On the one hand we have this carcass of an old world that is dying. It is going through the death throes. And yet, here is this new world that has already been born, and is growing and is going to continue for thousands of years. It isn't going to be the end of the world: it is the *end of an old world* and the *simultaneous establishment of a new one*. We are already in the early stages of the golden era of the human race." [135]

It is so very true when Dr. Greer shares that "the entirety of creation is sacred and every being is sacred, because spirit, the awake Being, is the very fabric of all that there is. And it is always perfectly one, even if it's playing and displaying upon itself as if it is different. The challenge is to see the

---

[135] Greer, Steven. (2006). *Hidden Truth: Forbidden Knowledge* (p 226). Crozet, VA: Crossing Point, Inc.

oneness within the difference, and also enjoy the difference." [136]

(5) *Follow your bliss.*

Author Joseph Campbell, now deceased, is responsible for these three profound words. Many have lived their very lives in keeping with this principle.

As one discovers what it is that makes them come alive, vibrating with intensity, feeling and passion, they will have found their bliss.

A voracious reader, I love to play with words on the written page.

A lover of history, I lose all track of time when engaged in research directly related to my own personal genealogies.

A disseminator of information, I attempt to share truth as per my Portals of Spirit website. Alternative healing modalities (crystals, meditation, healing layouts, Reiki) have become my way of giving back to myself and others, including Mother Gaia.

---

[136] Greer, Steven. (2006). *Hidden Truth: Forbidden Knowledge* (p 270). Crozet, VA: Crossing Point, Inc.

This is what constitutes my bliss. Do you know what your bliss is?

A few manipulate while billions allow themselves to be manipulated. The pertinent question to be asking in this situation is – where does the *real* responsibility lie?

We cannot be controlled unless we allow ourselves to be. The reality is that we are all One. Everyone else's freedom, then, becomes our own.

"When we get ourselves right, the world must come right because we are the world and the world is us. Society is the sum total of human thinking and feeling. It is a reflection of our attitudes. When we change them, we change society. We are only a change of mind away from real freedom, the freedom to express our God-given uniqueness and celebrate the diversity of gifts, perceptions and inspiration that exist within the collective human psyche." [137]

In keeping with an online article, entitled "Living With The Matrix or The Irreversible Effect of Developing Blue Pill Resistance" ...

---

[137] Icke, David. (1999). *The Biggest Secret* (p 493). Scottsdale, AZ: Bridge of Love Publications USA.

"One of the key scenes in "The Matrix" is when Neo, played by Keanu Reeves, has to choose between the blue and the red pill. Once he has taken the red pill, he no longer is fooled by the imaginary world the Matrix has created for its captives. He suddenly can recognize the Matrix for what it is and how it operates. While the Matrix in the movie is a machine that has trapped mankind in cocoons as a source of electrical energy, the Matrix in the real world has trapped us as a source of income in a world of taxes, interest rates, and consumerism.

"I can't decide which Matrix is worse, the one in the movie, or the one in the outside world. For generations now, we have been fooled into believing that we live in a world of freedom and human rights, where we elect our governments and are protected by the rule of law. We are told that in return for that privilege we have to pay tax, rent and interest, and, at times, go to war to protect this wonderful way of life.

"While the simpler minds amongst us are kept quiet with a modern version of ancient Rome's bread and games, the more educated people are filled with gigabytes of illusionary data, tricking them into believing they live in a world that only exists in their heads, meaning an enlightened society, where everything is so much better than in the Dark Ages of the past, where all are a big family, a caring society that

73

ensures that everybody is taken care of and nobody discriminated against.

"What worries me the most is how the ruling elite in recent years has decided that it no longer needs to be so 'caring'. It got cocky and felt that 'wasting' so much money on maintaining the illusion is no longer required. The big project of creating the New World Order is almost complete and the mind-control so powerful, our self chosen rulers, have decided that they can risk cutting down on welfare, public health and education, and all those other spoils that kept the masses happy after the debacle of World War II.

"Like in the movie, where taking the red pill suddenly allowed Neo to see through the Matrix, doing so in the real world has an irreversible effect. Once we realize that the world we live in is nothing but an illusion, the rest is just a matter of time. The real world, the world of the Matrix, is right in front of our eyes. The same data, be we 'blue pillers' or 'red pillers', means totally different things, and once we have seen the face of the evil machine, there is no turning back." [138]

---

[138] Winkler, Andrew. *Living With The Matrix or The Irreversible Effect of Developing Blue Pill Resistance.* Retrieved June 29, 2006, from

Having read this essay in its entirety, you may have come to the conclusion that I am an individual who approaches life from a negative standpoint. Let me share with you who I am.

I am a believer in the strength and tenacity of the human spirit, as has been evidenced, with clarity and sincerity, through Cathy O'Brien.

A believer in truth, such is what propels me to read, compile information and write, for it is only in coming to grips with truth that each person can endorse change. We can change things, but only beginning with our very selves. It only becomes in the changing of one's self that we are able to affect change on others.

I believe in complete and total disengagement from the Matrix as this is the truth-filled way to regaining what we have lost, what we have given away, what is rightfully ours, what has always been ours, and what we *must* take the time to reclaim.

Throughout this lengthy essay, I have merely reported what I have discovered.

---

http://www.ziopedia.org/en/articles/editorial/living_with_the_matrix_o
r_the_irreversible_effect_of_ developing_blue_pill_resistance/

As with all presented material, the reader must always use complete discernment in keeping with their own inner truths.

In conclusion, the time to reclaim one's personal power is now, for there is important work to be done.

Espavo.

Essay 2

Creating A More Positive Collective Reality

© March 2008 by Michele Doucette

Having written the previous essay to better inform the reader, so that all can work on actively disengaging from the Matrix, I have chosen to write this next installment, focusing on how one can *more effectively work towards changing themselves*, thereby changing their reality.

It becomes imperative, however, to understand that as long as one judges their own reality to be deficient in some way, they will never be able to change it because they have not accepted it for the lessons it may bring.

As long as you continue to judge, you merely get more of the same.

To evolve spiritually, you do not require any help outside of yourself. All you need can be found within. Take the time to get to know who you really are.

Seek (knowledge) *and ye shall find* (knowledge) for it is positive energy that nourishes the soul and truth that liberates.

Much of the research that I am delving into appears to hint at the same thing – that we are reality creators, that we are vibrational beings, that all is comprised of energy.

As shared in my previous essay, we create by way of thoughts, feelings and emotions, all of which resonate at a specific frequency.

Many have said, and continue to say, that in order to change the world, one must change themselves.

Much easier said than done, especially when we appear to be controlled by the "well-crafted, mind-boggling business of fear that has overrun the planet." [139]

How, then, do we go about releasing ourselves from this collective bondage of fear? How do we go about creating and maintaining a positive, more optimistic, mindset?

As more and more chaos appears to be unleashed, as events playing out on the world stage appear less and less stable, all of which results in the creation of mass confusion, many are experiencing an overwhelming desire to delve within, all in an attempt to better understand the reason(s) for our being here, on this planet, at this time.

"Understanding the power of beliefs and the power of the mind, both individually and en masse, is the most pressing and crucial issue for humankind to grasp." [140]

Marciniak succinctly shares that "developing the ability to become aware of what you think, feel, and speak, and structuring your life with pristine clarity through thought,

---

[139] Marciniak, Barbara. (2004). *Path of Empowerment: New Pleiadian Wisdom for a World in Chaos* (p 5). Novato, CA: New World Library.
[140] Ibid, p 5.

word, and deed are of essential importance for living an empowered life." [141]

"Likewise, accepting responsibility for the power you embody is the essential and most important lesson of this transformation." [142]

I, too, am seeking this same level of transformation, of self-empowerment. Clearly, this is where one must begin. An individual, and collective, first step, if you will.

Marciniak writes that "questioning everything – your life, your beliefs, and your world view – is the most essential part of the process of discovering your inherent power to create the world you meet. It takes great courage to question your existence, and even greater strength is required to know and recognize the truth when you see it." [143]

"For many millennia the people of Earth have been continuously creating their experience by default and

---

[141] Marciniak, Barbara. (2004). *Path of Empowerment: Nw Pleiadian Wisdom for a World in Chaos* (p 6). Novato, CA: New World Library.
[142] Ibid.
[143] Ibid, p 15.

neglect," [144] meaning that we have not had complete control over our own thoughts, feelings, desires and emotions.

"For many decades a very controlled and corrupt media has been directing the attention of the masses by uniformly reporting on a state of managed chaos, which is scripted and staged to produce mental confusion and fatigue. The relentless reporting and rehashing of catastrophic and traumatic events with images of despair and destruction repeatedly planted into the minds of the viewers, create supreme states of anxiety and are, in reality, a form of psychological warfare. Authorities play with truths, half-truths, deceptions, and lies to render you hopeless, feeling it is pointless to do anything – this now passes as "the" news, and it can rule your life." [145]

Ready for the next installment?

"When millions of people focus their attention upon listening to the same words, seeing the same pictures, and hearing the same descriptions, tremendous energy is generated and a massive thought-form is created. Thought-forms are vibrational blueprints that hold

---

[144] Marciniak, Barbara. (2004). *Path of Empowerment: New Pleiadian Wisdom for a World in Chaos* (p 21). Novato, CA: New World Library.
[145] Ibid, pp 30-31.

instructions for manifesting reality. The media captures your attention and then programs your imagination, essentially canceling out your unique creative drive to manifest your own reality as well as your desire to know yourself. You have been conditioned to believe that all you need to know can now be found in the wonderful world of electronic boxes and the information and entertainment they contain. When "the news" is slanted toward a message of continuous war, a state of despair and a sense of hopelessness are created. A paralysis of power takes hold because you become convinced that the only reality is what is described and prescribed by the authorities in the box. Reality is created and produced by each and every one of you, and those seeking to control the world have kept this knowledge a well-guarded secret." [146]

We have been told what to think, what to believe, how to act, what to say, and how to respond – all courtesy of our leaders. Not an accusation, this has been our current reality for thousands of years. We have settled for the status quo, *until now.*

---

[146] Marciniak, Barbara. (2004). *Path of Empowerment: New Pleiadian Wisdom for a World in Chaos* (p 31). Novato, CA: New World Library.

Just imagine the flip-side of what we have been told to think, in what we have been told to believe.

In wanting to venture forth, there are some very important questions that we must ask of ourselves.

Am I sure that I really want to go there?

Do I want to rattle the bars of my self-imposed cage?

Do I wish to expand my mind by thinking outside the box?

Do I wish to enhance my conscious awareness to include new vistas of information?

Do I wish to refine my individual frequency band, my personal energy signature?

Do I wish to fine tune my perceptions?

Do I wish to identify hidden meanings of life?

Do I wish to fully participate in life?

Do I wish to observe my interactions without judgment?

Do I wish to be awakened?

Do I wish to experience complete and total freedom?

In feeling a powerful impetus to do so, I know that I must.

Having long been controlled through fear and guilt, my heart tells me that it is time to forge ahead.

As to my bravery, only time will tell, as I strive to break free from an ancient spell that has been in place for thousands of years.

Marciniak says that "you must first learn to manage your attention in the here and now in order to become much more aware of the language of frequencies. Inner signals and messages are effortlessly and generously transmitted by everyone." [147]

Many are aware that love is the vital-force energy that sustains all life. We were created in love. We come from love. We are love.

In learning to both cultivate and feel a genuine love and appreciation for who we are in this physical embodiment, we are able to more fully connect with this energy, contributing our own version of this love frequency to this 3D reality.

---

[147] Marciniak, Barbara. (2004). *Path of Empowerment: New Pleiadian Wisdom for a World in Chaos* (p 21). Novato, CA: New World Library.

So where does one actually start?

First and foremost, one starts by realizing that personal change is imminent. It then advances to positive thinking, something that is very difficult to achieve.

How can this be so, you ask?

"A positive outlook is a symptom of maturity, which takes time and conscious effort to develop. You have to uproot old attitudes and resolve deep-seated misunderstandings about life. As long as you feel angry, you can think wishful thoughts all you want, but nothing will happen. Positive thinking means learning to face the material in your shadows. You need to be whole inside if you want your affirmations to work." [148]

Muster continues by saying that "whenever you hold something in the spotlight of your awareness, you are using the power of the conscious mind. Thousands of thoughts go through your mind every day, like a raging river of thought. However, if you do not pay attention to what you think, you may waste this valuable resource dwelling on useless negative things like worry and gossip. If you want to use

---

[148] Muster, Nori. (2007). Dreaming Peace: Introduction.
Retrieved February 2, 2008, from
http://surrealist.org/writing/dreamingpeaceintro.html

the power of your mind for your benefit, you need to change your thoughts. To improve your thoughts, you first have to be aware of what they are. If you learn to change your mind through positive autosuggestion, you can change your reality too." [149]

Although becoming aware of your thoughts is a time consuming process, it is absolutely essential. Do not expect this to be an easy process. You must focus on taking baby steps, one day at a time, in an effort to counteract your thinking.

In essence, it is much akin to reconfiguring your brain whilst, at the same time, dismantling the ego, which is a painful process, even when one deems themselves ready and up to the challenge.

Where does the subconscious mind come into play in keeping with one's thoughts, you ask?

The subconscious tries to help by showing us the truth, attempting to communicate through our dreams and gut feelings, that, while painful, can be viewed as a trustworthy friend.

---

[149] Muster, Nori. (2007). How Positive Thinking Works, Part 1: Autosuggestion. Retrieved February 2, 2008, from http://surrealist.org/writing/dreamingpeace1.html

"The subconscious knows everything about you and records every thought, picture, and feeling you think. You need to be aware of your feelings and be responsible for them." [150]

In continuation, Muster shares that "it may be difficult to recognize the negative mental attitudes you have acquired. They may seem so familiar that you take them for granted. You may wake up with a vague feeling of foreboding. You may be overcome with worry or raw feelings about money. You may feel so angry about some aspect of your life that you can't imagine living without the anger. However, once you have some experience using autosuggestion, you will realize these are just thoughts in the mind ... deeply embedded patterns attached to neurons with negative programming. You can change them because you are the one who decides what thoughts to keep. You have the ability to change anything about your inner life if you make a conscious effort." [151]

---

[150] Muster, Nori. (2007). How Positive Thinking Works, Part 1: Autosuggestion. Retrieved February 2, 2008, from http://surrealist.org/writing/dreamingpeace1.html
[151] Muster, Nori. (2007). How Positive Thinking Works, Part 11: Positive Mental Attitude. Retrieved February 2, 2008, from http://surrealist.org/writing/dreamingpeace2.html

Let's face it. Mental attitudes are often difficult to change because they are generally based on one's underlying beliefs. To change and/or challenge one's mental attitude(s), to develop positive thinking, one must question their belief system(s), and most would rather not do so. It is a painful, but necessary, process.

Muster discusses negative mental states (all of which embody such things as fear, unproductive worrying, excessive worrying, perfectionism, jealousy, anger, resentment, chronic victim hood, loneliness, emptiness and superstitions) in greater depth, all of which can control one to such a degree that they become completely paralyzed.

Love is an exceptionally big part of positive thinking. You have to both love and accept yourself, all facets of yourself, the light as well as the dark, in order to begin experiencing what has been referred to as your higher purpose.

In keeping, interpersonal relationships also figure into positive thinking, and, yet one also has to learn to be themselves, to learn to remain true to who they are by listening to their heart, in order to most effectively deal with a situation that may arise. If one tries to blend in and/or conform to the expectations of another, such will simply consign themselves to 'mediocrity' as shared by Muster.

In having entered the love paradigm and/or positive thinking paradigm, which may be a complete paradigm shift for some people, you continue to set an example for others.

"Although things may look bleak ... with endless wars, the threat of terrorism, diminishing natural resources, catastrophic weather events ... good things can happen too. There are tremendous challenges, but when enough people hold a vision of love, it will happen." [152]

If indeed "we want to create a peaceful world, then we must set an example of what it is like to live by peaceful ideals. In the peace paradigm, humanity is one people and everyone is part of the whole." [153]

Raised within the Catholic faith, like Steve Pavlina, I was able to reprogram my religious beliefs, a process that spanned years.

I began my Gnostic search, seeking my own inner truth based on what resonated within the core of my being.

---

[152] Muster, Nori. (2007). How Positive Thinking Works, Part IV: Solve Collective Problems. Retrieved February 2, 2008, from http://surrealist.org/writing/dreamingpeace4.html
[153] Ibid.

Delving into the so-called New Age realm, I ended up taking a bit from many disciplines in order to create my new belief system. Almost immediately, I began attracting like-minded individuals into my life.

It was likewise for Pavlina who shares that he came to understand that "instead of your beliefs being based on reality, they're creating your reality." [154]

Things begin to get more interesting when Pavlina says that "I can't prove to you that you're in a thought bubble right now. But you can prove it to yourself if you have enough curiosity to make the attempt. You have to decide to swallow the red pill. The only way to prove you're in a thought bubble is to consciously change your thoughts in such a way that you contradict at least one of the foundational beliefs that form the bubble. This begins with opening your mind to the possibility that your thoughts are shaping your reality." [155]

---

[154] Pavlina, Steve. (2005). Take the Red Pill. Retrieved February 2, 2008, from http://www.stevepavlina.com/blog/2005/03/take-the-red-pill/
[155] Ibid.

In stepping outside the preconceived beliefs as governed by the Matrix, one is able to completely contradict many foundational beliefs that exist within this controlled environment.

"To what degree do our thoughts create our reality? That I don't know. I'm convinced beyond a reasonable doubt that our thoughts have a strong and powerful effect on creating the reality we experience. But I don't know how strong this factor is. I don't know how deep the rabbit hole goes. I'm sitting in a thought bubble of my own, and as such my own reality is being shaped by the nature of that bubble." [156]

As per the discussed Brotherhood Agenda in reference to my previous essay, *Our Current Collective Reality Is Most Shocking Indeed*, we have allowed ourselves to be manipulated by such institutions such as religion, politics, education and science.

As long as one completely adheres to rigid dogma and a closed mind, one can never take back their power.

---

[156] Pavlina, Steve. (2005). Take the Red Pill. Retrieved February 2, 2008, from http://www.stevepavlina.com/blog/2005/03/take-the-red-pill/

Coming to the realization that "if you created the present reality that you don't like, you can just as easily create a new reality that you do" [157] is heady stuff.

"You are in control. You have all the answers. You are the centre of your own universe and you can make it whatever you choose. You are simply incredible. Feel it, live it and your world will be transformed." [158]

Now is the time to reclaim the power that we have given away. How does one, therefore, go about reclaiming this power so as to begin thinking anew for themselves?

David Icke makes note of several noteworthy steps.

"Step One – Refuse to have another tell you what to think and do with your life. What matters is that you are you and not what someone else is telling you to be. Respect the freedom of others to do the same." [159]

Remain true to yourself by listening to your heart.

---

[157] Icke, David. (1999). *The Biggest Secret* (p 488). Scottsdale, AZ: Bridge of Love Publications USA.
[158] Ibid.
[159] Ibid, p 444.

"Step Two – As the process of unplugging continues, things that mattered to you before become less important and your outlook on life and others starts to transform. You become more tolerant of yourself and others. Your attitudes to everything change once the recognition of the illusion goes deeper and deeper and you start to be that awareness rather than just intellectually accepting its existence. Don't think it, know it. Don't try to do it, just do it. These are very different states of being. When you become more consciously aware of the illusion, you can begin to enjoy it without all the hang-ups that imprison us when we think it is real. We can have fun and express our desires, as long as they don't impinge on the freedom of others." [160]

Live and partake of the now. Cease the unproductive and unnecessary worry. Trust in the greater power of the Universe.

"Step Three – Taking ... responsibility and ceasing to blame others – or ourselves come to that – is to take a massive step on the freedom road. The power the Illuminati use to control and manipulate is only the power we give away to them and others every day. The most destructive expression of this is blaming others for our plight. In truth, only we have that

[160] Icke, David. (2003). *Tales from The Time Loop* (pp 445-448). Wildwood, MO: Bridge of Love Publications USA.

power if we choose to use it; but if we believe that others are in control of our destiny we will create that reality.

"Step Four – We need to start focusing on the right to freedom of expression" [161] for all.

As long as we believe that division and separateness exists, the Matrix has us and owns us, for it alone promotes this duality.

Oneness = Love = Balance

Hatred = Illusion of Division = Disharmony

Marciniak is in complete agreement.

"You can change any situation by changing your previous attitudes and expectations. Refocusing your attention and consciously selecting your thoughts to reinforce the outcome you desire will alter the frequency you transmit, inevitably opening the door to another probable outcome. Reality

---

[161] Icke, David. (2003). *Tales from The Time Loop* (pp 445-448). Wildwood, MO: Bridge of Love Publications USA.

adjusting, or using your frequency by way of intent, is the wave of the future." [162]

When we focus on something, we give power to the vibrations. In essence, these ideas ultimately become our truth. This is true for both positive and negative thoughts. You simply end up creating more of the same, depending on the nature of your focus.

What we believe, we bring into being. By focusing on abundance rather than lack, we can enjoy a reality in alignment with positive energies and new beginnings.

If we want to see more love in the world, we must become love. If we want to see more peace in this world, we must become peace. If we want to see more compassion in this world, we must become compassion. Simply put, we must become that which we seek.

Unplugging from the Matrix, from the illusion that we have long considered real, is not an easy road for most. What does it involve?

---

[162] Marciniak, Barbara. (2004). *Path of Empowerment: New Pleiadian Wisdom for a World in Chaos* (p 50). Novato, CA: New World Library.

No problem can be solved from the same level of consciousness that created it. These powerful words were uttered by Albert Einstein.

"There are a number of versions of what Einstein is supposed to have said, but this one encapsulates all of them. In short, the problems that we see in this world, this *reality*, cannot be repaired by the same kind of thinking, sense of reality, that created them. Why? Because the 'world' is a reflection of that 'thinking' and if the 'thinking' doesn't change, neither can its reflection: the 'world'. The manipulators understand this and they are constantly offering and encouraging 'solutions' that they know will just exacerbate the problems and create more." [163]

"Round and round we go and so it must be because the global merry-go-round is just a manifestation of thought processes, individual and collective, going round and round, repeating, repeating, repeating. As the saying goes – If you always do what you've always done, you'll always get what you've always got. Put another way – If you think what

----

[163] David Icke Newsletter. Received via email on February 3, 2008, from http://www.davidicke.com/

you've always thought, you'll create what you've always created." [164]

Unless one wants to be stuck in the same mindset day after day, year after year, lifetime after lifetime, a consciousness shift, outside of the ever repeating cycle [meaning that we are trying to solve problems with the same level of consciousness that created them], is needed in order to trigger any transformation of the current reality.

"True Love ... has a different agenda. True Love creates reality and True Love creates opportunities. Trust in the voice of your beloved one inside your heart. This voice never lies. Trust in yourself." [165]

In keeping, True Love is stronger than the Matrix system of control.

"Love in its true and infinite sense is not a spectator, not some inactive esoteric concept. It is the ultimate power in all existence and it is there for everyone to connect with and

---

[164] David Icke Newsletter. Received via email on February 3, 2008, from http://www.davidicke.com/

[165] The Rules of the Matrix. Retrieved on February 2, 2008, from http://www.geocities.com/freeyourbrain/rules.htm

express in daily experience whenever we choose. The tragic thing is that we *don't* choose and that's why we have the world that we do." [166]

Become Conscious. These two words will assist in the transformation of our current reality to something much more, to something that is equated with love and respect.

"These values are the soul mates of awakened consciousness and they will transform this ball of division and conflict into the paradise it is destined to be. Paradise is not a place, it is a state of being that transcends all places, races and expressions of the Infinite." [167]

In practical terms, this means "doing what you *know* to be right rather than what you *think* is right for you in the moment," [168] with right meaning in reference to your heart.

"What does the heart tell you is the right course of action? And let us not kid ourselves that we don't know what the heart is saying. We *do* – it's just that its urgings are ignored

---

[166] David Icke Newsletter. Received via email on February 3, 2008, from http://www.davidicke.com/
[167] Ibid.
[168] Ibid.

because the head is saying: What are the consequences here for me?" [169]

It is the system, also known as the Matrix, that urges us to put the self first. By comparison, love urges us to see that "we are all One and that therefore the greater good and the 'individual' good are indivisible." [170]

Just imagine "the transformation of daily life that would emerge from the values of love and doing what we *know to be right* and not what we think is right for us. Unfairness and injustice would fade away and so would conflict, war and imposition of will." [171]

There will be times when "it will be right to defend yourself against injustice and stand your ground in the name of fairness. Other times it will be right to concede your own position and desires to provide fairness and justice for another." [172]

---

[169] David Icke Newsletter. Received via email on February 3, 2008, from http://www.davidicke.com/
[170] Ibid.
[171] Ibid.
[172] Ibid.

The question then becomes how do we create such a world? We begin by engaging in a completely different state of being by doing what we *know* to be right and fair.

In essence, *we become conscious*, and in so doing demonstrate opening the channels to higher consciousness. The energy that is carried by our intent "cracks the auric eggshells of body consciousness and sets us free of the system's 'values' that are designed to enslave us in me, me, me." [173]

Are you now beginning to envision what the gifts of love and respect can give to the world, "a world in which everyone does what they like as long as they don't impose it on anyone else. Diversity of view and lifestyle can live in harmony so long as love and respect hold the balance between them. It brings together both respect for our right to do and be what we choose while respecting those same rights for others and it will bring an end to the complexity that engulfs us today," [174] keeping us prisoner.

_____

[173] David Icke Newsletter. Received via email on February 3, 2008, from http://www.davidicke.com/
[174] Ibid.

The system loves complexity because it entraps the mind. We remain bewildered in that the problems are too big and there is nothing that we can do, leading to inaction.

Can any of this be accomplished with the level of today's collective consciousness?

Once again, we are back to Albert Einstein for our answer: *No problem can be solved from the same level of consciousness that created it.*

On the flip side, nor can "a reality be transformed by the same level of consciousness that enslaved it." [175]

The consciousness shift that is needed is coming. We are awakening to a new point of observation.

The biggest challenge for all of us in this time of much needed transition is to live our words and not just speak them.

Humans have developed a wondrous gift for self-deception and we are simply brilliant at persuading ourselves that what we think is right for us is what is right for the greater good. It is time to be honest with ourselves.

---

[175] David Icke Newsletter. Received via email on February 3, 2008, from http://www.davidicke.com/

Eckhart Tolle, author of *A New Earth: Awakening To Your Life's Purpose*, was the forefront guest on Oprah, courtesy of a live world wide web event. Throughout these online sessions, with the first class airing on Monday, March 3, 2008, Oprah and Eckhart were exploring the concept(s) found within the book.

No matter where in the world you were living at that time, you were able to participate, courtesy of your computer.

I completely acknowledge and concur with The Big Lie (both *attachment to the ego* as well as *separation from the Infinite Source*) that we have been fed in this current dreamstate for thousands and thousands of years, the basis of *Our Current Collective Reality Is Most Shocking Indeed*, my previous essay. In keeping, I made a conscious decision to reclaim my power.

I am currently able to observe my own thoughts within a much increased state of detached neutrality, only because I had to learn to reconfigure my thoughts, my words, my reactions; a process that took years.

No longer asleep, I can completely attest to the fact that when one begins to get out of their own way (the dissolving of the ego), they begin to develop a trust beyond who they thought they once were.

As Eckhart Tolle states, it is this refinement that will serve to change the collective consciousness of the planet.

All of the individual fears, doubts, angers, jealousies and resentments contribute to the collective consciousness. In keeping, therefore, each individual must step out of their own egoic consciousness, in order to begin to change themselves.

In so doing, they also begin to change the collective. Even the tiniest ripple can elicit a wave of change.

My focus has since become needing to reach that place within that is unconditioned and formless (spirit), inviting stillness into my life.

I am no longer as interested in worldly things. Although I am not sure where this will take me, I am willing to step out of my own way in order to continue to learn see with enhanced clarity.

For the true power within to shine forth, the ego has to die. One is then resurrected and reconnected with their very soul.

Could this be what has long been meant by the cryptic, and very much paraphrased, words attributed to Jesus – the importance of living in the world and yet not being a part of the world?

In each of the sixteen chapters of this book, "one special word is written with something different about its presentation ... NoT misprints or typing errors ... but intentionally altered or 'coded' to spell out a special message." [176] In keeping, "those persons who search and record them in the order presented will find revealed a deep ancient secret that was extracted from the ancient *Book of God*, a mysterious old document written on a fabric of an unknown nature, and highly regarded by the Ancients thousands of years ago." [177]

It is further shared that these "coded clues are called *Words of Truth* and there is no glamorous earthly prize for their discovery, excepting hidden treasure to nourish the Soul." [178]

Herein lies the special message contained within the text.

Learn deeply of the mind and its mystery for therein lies the true secret of immortality.

This clearly means that we need not look outside of ourselves for the answers that we seek. All that we need resides within. One merely needs to embrace the silence,

---

[176] Bushby, Tony. (2003). *The Secret In The Bible* (p 6). Queensland, Australia: Joshua Books.
[177] Ibid.
[178] Ibid.

the stillness, the unconditioned, the formless, the spirit, the void, in order to go to the place where the mind is no longer operating. A place where all is still without thinking, where one will be able to reconnect with the very essence and sacredness of their being, and that can only be reached by being still. Eckhart Tolle shares that this is a place where you are more alert than when you are thinking.

Spirituality has *nothing* to do with what you believe and *everything* to do with your state of consciousness.

The basis for all life is the present moment. Acceptance of the moment as it is. Gratitude is also a significant part of this enhanced awareness.

In speaking for myself, I am ready to be still. I am ready to be present in the moment; to be at peace with what is.

"It doesn't matter if an individual cannot alter the world or individually change the System. What matters is that whatever the individual does, they do it from the heart, with loving intent. Only then will changes become noticeable. Only then will the individual begin to tap into their true source of power – that which lies within. If we do not tap into this inner core, we will never synchronize with our true potential, and that unique inspiration will never come to the fore to be realized and worked with. Until that happens we will always be manipulated by whoever has the will to control us. We will always be 'followers' and clones, reactionary beings, and not what we are supposed to be: unique creators and channels for the Source into this world of matter." [179]

Fraser goes onto say that "the only advice I am going to give is advice which I believe will empower people to find their own power. From that position comes enlightenment. With enlightenment comes escape from the reliance on others because at the end of the day all evolution and creation comes from within." [180]

"1. Look upon every man, woman and child as your equal. We are all from the same Source, and your love for them will help them to harmonize with yours and their inner spirit which is One in the Source.

"2. Respect their right to individuality. You don't have to agree with them. You don't even have to like what they do or believe. However you respond to what they do or what they stand for, never lose sight of the fact that you and they are spiritual kin. We have a right not to agree and to dislike

---

[179] Fraser, Ivan. "Love Changes Everything". The Truth Campaign magazine. September 2000: Volume 17, p 49.
[180] Ibid.

another's actions and beliefs. But to hate another is like hating a part of one's own body.

"3. Love yourself. This will plug your awareness into your heart center. It will enable clarity of thought and perception. The ultimate realization here is the fact that by truly loving another, you are loving yourself.

"4. Make everything you do a dedication to the affirmation: May this be for *the greater good of all*. When you affirm this make sure it is drawn from within in accordance with The Source of All Truth and Light." [181]

"5. Remember, you have absolute freewill. That freewill includes the opportunity to choose to live in service for the greater good of all. You don't have to become a martyr. Just become who and what you already are and align with the Source in your daily life.

"6. Choose to live according to the heart first rather than the head first. The two need to be balanced, and spirit must be grounded, but the heart knows far more than the head and if trusted can lead to remarkably wonderful synchronicities

---

[181] Fraser, Ivan. "Love Changes Everything". The Truth Campaign magazine. September 2000: Volume 17, pp 49-50.

and realizations. The inner spirit is your connection with the Source, the Godhead.

"7. Of course, there must be a degree of sacrifice. We cannot gain without giving and we cannot take just because we want, for it is the over-stimulation of 'want' which has led us to become so out of balance with our true selves. Over-stimulated want comes from the desire to control and this comes from the need of the ego. And the ego must always be kept in check and guided by our inner awareness. When the heart says 'give' then it is time to give, so give generously of your time and energy to others who need it. But do not do it to the detriment of yourself – which you will not if you love and respect yourself as much as you love and respect others.

"8. Appreciate everyday what you have.

"9. Remember to find time to be still and quiet to allow the inner voice to speak to you.

"10. Speak your truth openly and do not fear what others may think of you in consequence. Avoid lying to others as lies create imbalance and carry karmic energy which eventually rebounds upon the liar.

"11. Face every adversity as a learning experience. Only you can decide whether an experience is there to face or avoid. Only love of the self and others will bring forth the realization of how to deal with any situation correctly.

"12. Never allow guilt to interfere with your life. If you have erred, learn from it and give thanks to yourself for the opportunity you have given yourself to learn and evolve.

"13. Harm none as much as is humanly possible and do as you will." [182]

I, too, see these as being extremely important rules to live by.

Caught up in the web of competition, greed, jealousy, envy and hate, we have been lost to ourselves for a very long time. As the ultimate driver of one's life, we have been asleep at the wheel for far too long. We have completely forgotten who we are.

We have forgotten how to celebrate the expanse and greatness of all life. As one awakens and become more aware, life is filled with the vibrations of love, peace, joy, wisdom and harmony.

---

[182] Fraser, Ivan. "Love Changes Everything". The Truth Campaign magazine. September 2000: Volume 17, pp 50-51.

First experiencing and then emanating these very vibrations, it is in the focusing on them that one is able to more readily re-discover who they really are.

It is in remembering our connection to all others, that we can more fully understand how revisions in attitudes and thought patterns can affect all that is around us.

The entirety of creation is sacred. The challenge is to see the oneness that all share while enjoying the individualistic differences. As the Buddha said, *you cannot do violence to another when you realize oneness.*

We are extensions of the Creator. In this light, we are all creator gods. However, long have we allowed other creator gods to create for us. As a result of not thinking and taking responsibility for ourselves, such is what has led to the fear, anxiety, despondency and chaos that is prevalent today.

It will be in the conquering of our own fears that positive frequencies will be able to overtake what has dominated for too long, making it easier to begin to hold, keep and maintain this new pulsation while also *living* it.

As one lives their frequency, they affect everyone in like manner, including Mother Gaia.

Listen to your inner being. Discover your reality from the *inside*, thereby directing your life in this way. What gets very difficult at times, as emotions are involved, is allowing tyranny to take place.

Everyone is endowed with the potential to create their own reality, even if it does not mirror your own.

Most people on the planet, however, allow others to create and dictate their reality to them. In this manner, we have been encouraged to look outside of ourselves for the answers.

As you begin to live according to your own guidance, daring to break free from the Matrix, everything changes to the extent that one becomes empowered when their emotions are no longer entangled with the Matrix that currently exists.

It is important to remember that in citing the Matrix, I am referring to those who create and dictate the reality for the multitude, the place where darkness has been reigning.

It becomes my role to love and honor the Divine being that I am. Just as a wise parent must allow their child to grow through their own experiences, so, too, does the Creator allow us our free will to evolve in this way.

I must resume, and assume, my own authority so as to lesson the complacency that currently exists on the planet. It, therefore, becomes my role to both trust my own identity as well as personal experiences with synchronicity.

In my desire to begin evolving, I made the conscious decision to become media free. I do not read the newspaper. I do not read news related magazines. I do not listen to the radio. I do not watch television.

A process that spanned years, I knew this to be the only way for me to begin disengaging myself from the constant frequency of chaos, anxiety and stress that is prevalent on the planet.

I began to listen to what was going on inside of myself, living in the world but yet not part of the emotional entanglement (which is where one can be hopelessly lost to the Self).

Now that I have experienced success in maintaining a significant level of neutrality, there are times when I may decide to inform myself as to world happenings.

Knowing that we are being controlled through our emotions, this is where the break must come. Maintaining neutrality is of extreme importance as this is what serves to bring one to a place of empowerment.

When you operate at a level of total sovereignty, those who wish to control you are not interested in you for the simple fact that they want a fearful, chaotic frequency, as this is what continues to give them power and control.

"Fear and chaos have predominated on this planet because these entities have stirred them up. They have divided and conquered everywhere to create that frequency. When you operate in peace and love and with information, you alter the structure of this place drastically: you bring choice of frequency back to this planet." [183]

As mentioned previously, the education system is another area where we are being controlled. The completion of my Masters program confirmed this on many levels. As an educator, this is something that I find myself continuously wrestling with on a day-to-day basis.

It is becoming more and more imperative that we must learn to read energies, using more than our five senses to perceive reality as they merely serve to limit one's perceptions of reality. Now is the time to begin relying on other forms of sensing, such as our knowing, intuitive, *feeling*, psychic self.

---

[183] Marciniak, Barbara. (1992). *Bringers of the Dawn: Teachings from the Pleiadians* (p 96). Rochester, VT: Bear & Company Publishing.

When one re-discovers their own way of intuiting, their own knowledge, they can no longer be controlled through fearful frequencies.

"When a human being resonates electromagnetically and broadcasts the frequency of fear, a transmission of consciousness is sent out. Where does that fear go? Where do your thoughts go? Where do your emotions go?" [184]

These are pertinent questions, to be sure. How many of us have ever really meditated and deliberated on the answers?

In awakening each morning, take the time to clearly state what you intend to experience throughout the day. Herein lies the beginning to establishing one's reality for it is thought that creates experience and experience that creates reality.

Your experience is *always* a direct reflection of what you are thinking. Your thoughts form your world *all* of the time.

As there exist so many frequency-control vibrations, you must remain clear and centered as to your thoughts, living in the now.

---

[184] Marciniak, Barbara. (1992). *Bringers of the Dawn: Teachings from the Pleiadians* (p 113). Rochester, VT: Bear & Company Publishing.

"You are a result of your thoughts. Thought creates experience. Why not give yourself a gift and begin to think of yourself in a capacity that is exceptional, magnificent, and uplifting." [185]

One's words can be either empowering or disempowering. It is important to eliminate the words *should* and *trying* from your vocabulary.

Should implies that you are operating under someone else's sovereignty.

Trying does not mean the same as doing. Whenever you use the word *trying*, you will not accomplish anything because trying is an excuse.

Focus instead on these thoughts. I am a *doer*. I am a *manifestor*. There is *no limitation* on this planet.

I am living my life in accordance with the light (which means that my frequency vibration is rising).

In so doing, I am also altering the frequency of the planet.

---

[185] Marciniak, Barbara. (1992). *Bringers of the Dawn: Teachings from the Pleiadians* (p 121). Rochester, VT: Bear & Company Publishing.

"There is nothing stronger than your commitment to the exalted self. Once you commit yourself to the energy of light. The energy of exaltation, and uplifted frequency, you are marked." [186]

First and foremost, live your light with courage. Speak what you know without getting caught up in the drama.

"What does it mean to trust? It means to have such inner knowing that your thoughts create your world – to simply be quite certain, with divine nonchalance and inner knowing, that *if you think something, it is*." [187]

"Information is light; light is information. The more you become informed, the more you alter your frequency. You are electromagnetic creatures, and everything that you are, you broadcast to someone else." [188]

I am here to evolve myself to the highest capability within this human form. In so doing, I will also be affecting those around me in a positive way.

---

[186] Marciniak, Barbara. (1992). *Bringers of the Dawn: Teachings from the Pleiadians* (p 132). Rochester, VT: Bear & Company Publishing.
[187] Ibid, p 135.
[188] Ibid, p 140.

"Once you can consistently maintain a frequency of information and not be riding the roller coaster of emotions up and down because you don't know who you are, you will be given a task. Your blueprint is your own personal detailed plan or outline of action for this lifetime." [189]

"If you go into a meditative state, you will receive a picture of your identity and reality and the next step of your assignment day by day. Meditation is a way to get informed and to go to a place that nourishes you. You will move into your purpose and, more than likely, it will have to do with facilitating the frequency: transducing it, stepping it down to others, explaining it, using it to heal others, and stabilizing it for the human race. When each of you can hold a frequency of information without freaking out and can be counted upon to be consistent, then you anchor the frequency on the planet. That frequency is recognized. It cannot be traced, exactly, but it can be recognized. That is why there has been a frenzied step-up to alter that frequency. You will see more frequency control everywhere you look, only now you will be able to recognize it for what it is." [190]

---

[189] Marciniak, Barbara. (1992). *Bringers of the Dawn: Teachings from the Pleiadians* (pp 140-141). Rochester, VT: Bear & Company Publishing.
[190] Ibid, p 141.

Stay focused on your own growth, your own path, your own self. Do not overly concern yourself with what others are doing.

The Female version of self is equated with intuition, receptivity, creativity, compassion, nourishment, whereas the Male version of self is attributed with powerful, rational, intellectual. You are looking for the *integration of the male and female essence* within yourself. They make one whole.

We learn from experience, thereby arriving at a place where we truly value our uniqueness. The Hermit, has traveled the path, gaining wisdom and insight. Standing alone, holding the lantern that reveals, most knowingly, that the answers sought, the higher calling and sense of purpose, lies within one's own soul.

The answers that we are looking for can never be found by looking outside of ourselves to other people, to other situations. Out of necessity, we must connect with our inner spirit, putting the conditioning of the outside world aside in order to figure out what we believe in, what we choose to stand for.

It took some time for me to come to terms with the fact that focusing on one's personal needs is not being selfish.

How can one feel that they are an effective parent, spouse, teacher or friend if they are not feeling secure and/or fulfilled within themselves?

It is also of the utmost importance that we never lose sight of our goals, and, as always, continue moving towards our highest aspirations. One cannot exist indefinitely in the planning stages.

Growth requires action. In this light, it is important to do whatever it takes to maintain one's enthusiasm in order to remain true to their purpose.

When we are truly passionate about a goal, the energy to achieve it will follow. That being said, it is also important to acknowledge that one's choices often have long-term and even lifetime rewards and/or consequences; hence, it is important to make balanced decisions by way of careful considerations.

Knowledge is power. It is important, therefore, to educate oneself on a continuous basis, refusing to meekly accept that which is spoon fed to the multitude.

When one is on a quest for truth, it is always important to look below the surface. Important decisions are better made when one is able to distance themselves from drama, using strategy as opposed to reacting to events.

In making happiness and peace a conscious choice, such is where our true power lies.

Read with discernment. It is important to come at things from many different angles. See what resonates with you, what feels right. It is up to each to decide what to do with the information that comes to the fore as each individual is in charge of their own life.

Find what it is that you know, not what you want to believe or what you have been told. *Trusting what you know is imperative.*

When you trust what you know, you are activating that part of you that is connected to the Creator.

It is high time that we come back to that intuitive side of ourselves that has long been forgotten due to the emphasis placed solely on the logical.

All we need to know resides within.

We have but to remember; hence, we must find ourselves amidst the ego trappings of the physical.

In making personal choices, I am responsible for my actions.

I am learning the importance of choosing to work for the highest good of the whole, as opposed to myself, and yet there also comes the responsibility of realizing that one must avoid infringing upon the rights of another.

"We want you to become sovereign to yourself in a greater capacity, and to worship no one. The principles that you are to honor above all else are your physical vehicle, Earth, and all of Earth's occupants. Honor your physical body as if you have been given an impeccable jewel, and act as if you own the most valuable creation in the universe. Honor Earth first and foremost. This is part of the assignment, and where your value lies." [191]

In reference to the accessing of knowledge, "it used to be that each individual who evolved and studied the mysteries had one teacher, and knowledge was passed down from teacher to apprentice in a long line of tradition." [192]

Today, however, "you become your own teacher by activating what is inside you, through *clear intent*, and by

[191] Marciniak, Barbara. (1994). *Earth: Pleiadian Keys to the Living Library* (p 33). Rochester, VT: Bear & Company Publishing.
[192] Ibid, p 55.

following the impulses and knowledge that accompany the process." [193]

The inner you communicates "continuously with a you that can be called your higher self, or your inner teacher. It is a version of you, invisible to your current perceptions, that nonetheless has a powerful influence. Your higher self is connected with a vista of reality in which there is a purpose to all you select to experience. Ideally, your higher self communicates this grander view to you by way of impulse, synchronicity, and emotion. It is up to *you* to translate your own messages and realize that, as you decree, reality conforms." [194]

"The training that you are receiving is from your inner teacher. You have a blueprint inside you that leads to a different pathway. You learn by following what is awakening from within. You will gain the greatest amount of knowledge through personal experience. Acknowledge that there is something for you to learn in every event you encounter in your life." [195]

---

[193] Marciniak, Barbara. (1994). *Earth: Pleiadian Keys to the Living Library* (p55). Rochester, VT: Bear & Company Publishing.
[194] Ibid, p 68.
[195] Ibid, p 72.

It is my belief that all of humanity is here to learn an important lesson: the realization that we are connected to all that exists.

We are magnificent beings. Remembering who we are will help to bring about the changes that are needed. Mind you, in order to do so, we have to get out of our own way.

Many are currently moving along the path towards Ascension, moving to a higher vibrational level that is also associated with the Christ Consciousness.

This is a level of awareness that "does not judge, does not criticize, coerce, tempt, does not condone, does not react negatively" for the Christ Consciousness is "true wisdom, Divine truth, true happiness, unconditional love and total perfection." [196]

Mastering the ego is key, but seeing and feeling only the beauty that exists, within the moment, is paramount.

---

[196] Crea. What is Christ Consciousness. Retrieved March 9, 2008, from http://www.lightascension.com/arts/christconsciousness.htm

Although it is back to the classroom for me, to learn how best to reach that place within that is unconditioned and formless (spirit), inviting stillness into my life, I trust that I will have provided the reader with a sense of direction that they, too, may be able to follow.

Having recently received information on two videos of significant importance ......

We Are All One Consciousness [197]

Even The Troops Are Waking Up [198]

...... clearly, we are all *one consciousness* experiencing itself subjectively.

May you, too, come to this same conclusion.

Espavo.

---

[197] http://www.davidicke.com/articles/media-and-appearances/36572-we-are-all-one-consciousness-human-race-get-off-your-knees
[198] http://www.davidicke.com/articles/media-and-appearances/36265-even-the-troops-are-waking-up-a-fantastic-video

Michele Doucette is webmistress of *Portals of Spirit*, a spirituality website whereby one will find links to (1) *The Enlightened Scribe*, (2) an ezine called *Gateway To The Soul*, (3) books of spiritual resonance as well as authors of metaphysical importance, (4) categories of interest from Angels to Zen, (5) up-to-date information as shared by a Quantum Healer, (6) affiliate programs and resources of personal significance, (7) healing resource advertisements and (8) spiritual news.

As a Level 2 Reiki Practitioner, she sends long distance Reiki to those who make the request, claiming only to be a *facilitator of the Universal Energy*, meaning that it is up to the individual(s) in question to use these energies in order to heal themselves.

Having also acquired a Crystal Healing Practitioner diploma (Stonebridge College in the UK), she is guardian to many from the mineral kingdom. In keeping, she has written *The Wisdom of Crystals* which, currently offered as an ebook on her website, shall soon be released in paperback.

The author of several other spiritual/metaphysical tomes; namely, *The Ultimate Enlightenment For 2012: All We Need Is Ourselves*, *Turn Off The TV: Turn On Your Mind* and *Veracity At Its Best*, all of which have been released as paperback editions through St. Clair Publications.

In addition, she has also written *A Travel in Time to Grand Pré*, a visionary metaphysical title that historically ties the descendants of Yeshua to modern day Nova Scotia.

Against the backdrop of 1754 Acadie, it was the blending of French Acadian history with current DNA testing that allowed for the weaving of this alchemical tale of time travel, romance and intrigue.

From Henry I Sinclair to the Merovingians, from the Cathari treasure at Montségur to the Knights Templar, this novel, together with the words of Yeshua as spoken at the height of his ministry, has the potential to inspire others; for it is herein that we learn how individuals can find their way, their truth(s), so as to live their lives to the fullest.